Virginia P. Richmond · Jason S. Wrench · James C. McCroskey

SCARED speechless

seventh edition

Communication Apprehension, Avoidance, & Effectiveness

Kendall Hunt
publishing company

www.kendallhunt.com
Send all inquiries to:
4050 Westmark Drive
Dubuque, IA 52004-1840
This book was previously published by: Pearson Education, Inc.

Copyright ©2018 by Kendall Hunt Publishing Company

Text Alone ISBN 978-1-5249-4957-0
Text with VoiceVibes ISBN 978-1-5249-4956-3

Published in the United States of America

Dedication

This edition of *Scared speechless: Communication apprehension,
avoidance, and effectiveness* is dedicated to the legacy of
Dr. James C. McCroskey. He was a mentor and friend
to so many in the field. He will be remembered by the discipline
for many reasons, but without his ground-breaking work in
the area of communication apprehension this book would not exist.

Brief Contents

Preface ix

1. An Overview of Human Communication 1

2. Shyness: The Behavior of Not Communicating 23

3. Scared Speechless: The Fear of Communication 41

4. Intercultural and Interethnic Communication Apprehension 67

5. Impact of Apprehension, Shyness, and Low Willingness to Communicate in Life 85

6. Communication Avoidance and Communication Effectiveness 109

7. Reducing Apprehension and Anxiety about Communication 125

Glossary 147
References 151
Appendices 165

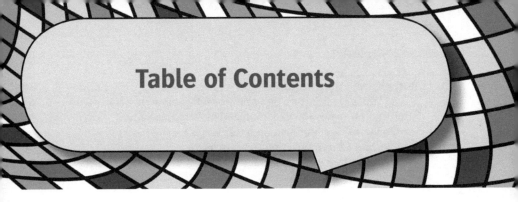

Table of Contents

Preface   ix

1. An Overview of Human Communication   1
    Definition of Human Communication   2
    Components of the Human Communication Process   4
    Functions of the Communication Process   12
    Misconceptions about Communication   14
        Misconception 1: Meanings are in the Words Themselves   14
        Misconception 2: Interpersonal Communication is the Same as
                           Intimate Communication   15
        Misconception 3: Communication is Solely a Verbal Process   17
        Misconception 4: Telling is Communicating   17
        Misconception 5: Communication will Solve All Our Problems   18
        Misconception 6: Communication is Always a Good Thing   18
        Misconception 7: The More Communication, the Better   19
        Misconception 8: Communication Can Break Down   19
        Misconception 9: Communication is a Natural Human Ability   20
        Misconception 10: Communication Competence Equals
                           Communication Effectiveness   20

2. Shyness: The Behavior of Not Communicating   23
    Individual Differences in Communication   23
    Effects of Individual Differences   26
    The Nature of Shyness   28
    The Causes of Shyness   29
    Types of Shy People   32
    Measures of Shyness   37

3. Scared Speechless: The Fear of Communication   41
    The Nature of Communication Apprehension   41
    The Biology of Fear   42
    Causes of Communication Apprehension   51
    Effects of Communication Apprehension   55
    Personality Correlates of Apprehension   57
    Compulsive Communicators   63

4. Intercultural and Interethnic Communication Apprehension   67
    The Influence of Culture on Communication Apprehension   67
    Cultural Influences on Communication Apprehension   75
    Intercultural Communication Apprehension   77
    Interethnic Communication Apprehension   79
    Communication Apprehension in Other Cultural Contexts   80
    Conclusion   82

5. Impact of Apprehension, Shyness, and Low Willingness to
    Communicate in Life   85
    Behaviors of Quiet and Talkative People   85
    Quiet vs. Talkative People: A Generalized Profile   91
    Interpersonal Perceptions   92
    Everyday Life   96
        Peer Relationships   96
        Family Relationships   97
        School Environment   98
        Work Environment   100
        Health Care   102
        Online   104
    Conclusion   106

6. Communication Avoidance and Communication Effectiveness   109
    Contributors to Communication Effectiveness   110
    Self-Perceived Communication Competence   112
    Sociocommunicative Style   113
    Immediacy   117

7. Reducing Apprehension and Anxiety about Communication   125
    Theories of Causes   125
    Treatment Approaches   130
    Samples of Nonthreatening to Threatening Communication
    Situations   135
    Summary   144

Glossary   147
References   151

Appendices
    A   Introversion Scale   165
    B   Shyness Scale   167
    C   Willingness to Communicate Scale (WTC)   169
    D   Writing Anxiety Scale (WAS)   171
    E   Singing Anxiety Test (SAT)   173
    F   Personal Report of Communication Apprehension-24 (PRCA-24) 175
    G   Personal Report of Public Speaking Anxiety (PRPSA)   177

H Communication Apprehension in Generalized Contexts 181
I Situational Communication Apprehension Measure (SCAM) 185
J Self-Perceived Communication Competence (SPCC) 187
K Talkaholism or Compulsive Communication 189
L Personal Report of Intercultural Communication
   Apprehension (PRICA) 191
M Personal Report of Interethnic Communication
   Apprehension (PRECA) 193
N Religious Communication Apprehension (RCA) 195
O Sociocommunicative Orientation 197
P Fear of Physician (FOP) 199
Q Computer-Mediated Communication Apprehension (CMCA) 201

Preface

This text provides an introduction to the process of human communication. Perhaps more important, it explains why you might fear communication situations. This text is for those of you who know people who are "scared speechless" and for those of you who are also scared speechless in some or most environments.

Chapter 1 offers a general foundation for understanding communication and discusses the basic components that make up the human communication process and the misconceptions and misunderstandings regarding the nature of communication. Chapter 2 focuses on shyness, the most widespread communication problem in our society, defining the problem and exploring why it occurs. Chapter 3 centers on communication apprehension, willingness to communicate, and the primary types of shyness. Chapter 4 examines the impact that one's culture can have on communication apprehension and how communication apprehension affects intercultural communication.

Chapter 5 summarizes some major effects of communication apprehension, willingness to communicate, and shyness in people's everyday lives and considers the problems of compulsive communicators. Chapter 6 centers on the effects of apprehension, avoidance, and willingness to communicate on communication effectiveness. The final chapter, Chapter 7, explains the various methods that have been developed to help people overcome apprehension and anxiety about communicating. This chapter gives guidance to persons who are scared about communicating with others.

A brief text such as this cannot include all the information you might wish to read about this subject. Consequently, we have included numerous references to help you pursue more in-depth knowledge. If you're looking for a more general introduction to the field of human communication, we would encourage you to look at our book *Human communication in everyday life: Explanations and applications* (Wrench, McCroskey, & Richmond, 2008). If you are particularly interested in communication apprehension and avoidance and willingness to communicate, we suggest you read *Avoiding communication: Shyness, reticence, and communication apprehension* (eds. Daly, McCroskey, Ayres, Hopf, Sonandre, &

Wongprasert, 2009). Daly et al. (2009) includes chapters written by many of the leading researchers in the area and provides more complete summaries of the relevant information than we can provide here. You should also read McCroskey and Richmond's chapter on "Willingness to communicate" in McCroskey, Daly, Martin, and Beatty's (1998) book *Communication and personality: Trait perspectives.*

CHAPTER 1
An Overview of Human Communication

Scared speechless!? If you're like many Americans, some aspect of communication (primarily public speaking) is enough to make you queasy in the knees, turn red, and give you sweaty palms and a dry mouth. Many people become anxious if not downright frightened when the prospect of speaking in public is even discussed. In a study conducted by Bruskin/Goldring Research (1993), a team of researchers examined the top-ten fears in North American adults:

10. Driving/riding in a car
9. Flying
8. Loneliness
7. Insects and bugs
6. Sickness
5. Death
4. Deep water
3. Heights
2. Financial problems
1. Speaking before a group

These findings ultimately led comedian Jerry Seinfeld to quote, "According to most studies, people's number one fear is public speaking. Number two is death. Death is number two. Does that sound right? This means to the average person, if you go to a funeral, you're better off in the casket than doing the eulogy." Although Seinfeld may have mixed up the numbers in this joke, the principle is still the same. There are lots of people in our society who are simply scared speechless. Most people think of anxiety in terms of public speaking, decades of research by communication scholars have found that anxiety while communicating can take on many different forms, which we will discuss throughout this book. For now, let's start by examining the nature of human communication.

In this age of technological advancements and increased attention to communication between people mediated by computers, smart phones, and iPads (and other tablets), it might seem as if human-to-human communication is less important than it used to be. This is not the case. Regardless of the new emphasis on computer-mediated communication, most of our daily interaction is with people on an interpersonal level. Supervisors still communicate with their subordinates on a one-to-one basis; teachers still communicate with students on a one-to-one basis; patients still communicate with their physicians or therapists on a one-to-one basis; and lovers still communicate with each other on a one-to-one basis. Thus, even though technology plays and will continue to play a significant role in our lives, technology cannot replace basic human interaction. Technology is increasingly utilized in many organizations for transferring information because of efficiency and speed, one-to-one communication between humans will always remain.

Definition of Human Communication

Human communication is the process by which a person (or persons) stimulates meaning in the mind of another person (or persons) through the use of verbal and/or nonverbal messages.

This definition encompasses three types of communication: accidental, expressive, and rhetorical.

Accidental Communication

Accidental communication occurs when a person does not realize he has stimulated meaning in the mind of another. This happens more frequently than many people realize. How often have you stimulated meaning in the mind of another person without really trying to do so? For example, you attend a lecture, and about halfway through the lecture you yawn several times. The speaker notices this and says something to the audience to the effect of, "I must be communicating something boring, the person in the back row yawned four times in the last five minutes." Everyone laughs, and you are embarrassed, unaware you have communicated boredom.

Most scholars in nonverbal communication suggest that through our nonverbal behaviors we are often accidentally communicating meanings to others. People communicate their needs, interests, desires, likes, dislikes, and weaknesses without having the slightest desire to do so and often despite a definite desire not to do so. The way we walk, talk, dress, and present ourselves stimulates meaning in another's mind about who we are and what we are like. This is not only true in the United States, it is true all over the world. For example, in many parts of the Middle East it is customary to stand very close and breathe into the other person's face when communicating. Americans find this offensive and often offend their Middle Eastern counterparts by backing away during an interaction. The American perceives the Middle Easterner as rude and aggressive, and the Middle Easterner perceives the American as cold and distant. Therefore, intercultural business transactions often are conducted by skilled intermediaries so the parties involved do not communicate something they do not mean to communicate.

Expressive Communication

Expressive communication occurs from the emotional, or motivational, state of an individual and can be intentional or unintentional. The messages produced represent the individual's feelings at a given time. For example, when you strike an incorrect key on your computer keyboard and accidentally delete material, you might shout "Damn!" —an exclamation that would convey to another person you are displeased with your keyboarding skills. If another person, a *receiver,* is not present, expressive communication cannot occur—no meaning is produced by the message.

Another framework in which to view expressive communication is the content and relational levels of messages (Watzlawick, Beavin, & Jackson, 1967). The content component of a message is simply what we say; the words that make up the message. The relational component of a message expresses how we feel about the other person or our relationship with the other person; it indicates how the other person should interpret the message. For example, your roommate might make the statement, "It's 8 a.m." The content message is fairly straightforward, and a bystander could logically conclude that only the time of day is being communicated. You, however, have relational clues—previous interactions, familiarity with your roommate's tone of voice, body movements, and so on and realize that her or his message is, in fact, "Get out of the bathroom—you've been in there for an hour, and I'm going to be late for my 8:30 class!"

Of course, the relational level of communication can result in accidental communication. Although we have much control over our expressive communication, instances still may occur when our expressive communication conveys something we did not intend. For example, the way you look at your friend, set something down on your desk, or walk across the room may convey a message you did not intend to communicate. Many of us, however, are high self-monitors and often control our voices, movements, and gestures to convey a certain emotional state without communicating in an accidental mode.

Rhetorical Communication

Rhetorical communication is the process of a source specifically attempting to stimulate a particular meaning in the mind of the receiver by means of verbal and nonverbal messages. The source is an individual or a group from whom the message emanates. In order for the source to be success-ful, the receiver must receive and interpret the message according to the source's intentions.

Rhetorical communication is goal-directed. The source seeks to pro-duce in the mind of the receiver a specific meaning. In this type of com-munication, a source might attempt several ways to get her or his meaning into the receiver's mind. A source will continue transmitting messages until the receiver reacts the way the source thinks he or she should, or the source will simply give up.

Our understanding of the communication process would not be com-plete without viewing the components necessary for effective communica-tion. The following section is devoted to listing and defining the various components in the human communication process.

Components of the Human Communication Process

The process of human communication has seven essential components: source, message, channel, receiver, encoding, decoding, and feedback. Several models of communication have been developed to illustrate the relationships among these components. One of the first models, the Shannon–Weaver model, makes no reference to meaning; instead it rep-resents message-centered communication (see Figure 1.1). This model incorporates a source (such as a person) who puts a message into a trans-mitter (such as a computer) then transmits the message through a channel (such as a telephone wire) to a receiver. (Shannon and Weaver also include noise in their model. We will discuss noise later in this chapter.) Berlo developed the SMCR model of human communication (see Figure 1.2), which also includes the source, message channel, and receiver(s). In addi-tion, this model allows for all three types of meaning-centered communi-cation: accidental, expressive, and rhetorical. SMCR implies that noise is present; however, it is not pictorially represented.

The SMCR model considers five elements that might impact commu-nication between source and receivers: the participants' communication skills, attitudes, and knowledge; the social system of which they are a part; and their cultural environment. This model suggests the channel is composed of the five primary sensory systems: seeing, hearing, touching, smelling, and tasting.

Both models (Figures 1.1 and 1.2) are good initial attempts at outlin-ing and describing the components in the human communication pro-cess. Both, however, fall short. The Shannon–Weaver model overlooks the interaction that may take place between source and receiver and fails to focus on meaning stimulated by interactions. The Berlo model fails to

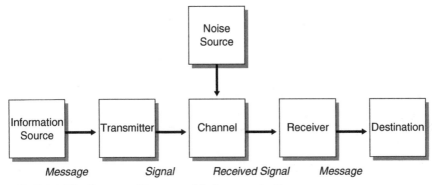

FIGURE 1.1 *The Shannon–Weaver model of communication*

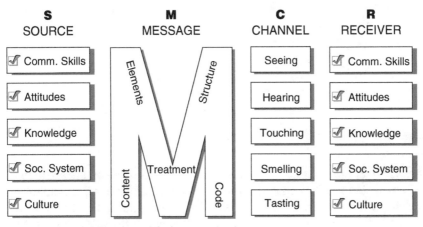

FIGURE 1.2 *Berlo's SMCR model of communication*

delineate communication as a process and overlooks the idea that receivers, not just sources, are active participants in the process. A source does not simply transmit a message with the receiver passively receiving it because receivers and sources act equally as participants in the human communication process. In addition, both models have left out other components that are important to the communication process, such as feedback. The most useful model for our purposes is the model presented in Figure 1.3. The Interpersonal Communication Model shows the basic interactive and often simultaneous-transactions communication model, which incorporates the process notion of communication. Below are some pointers that distinguish this model from other communication models and show the transactional, interactive nature of communication.

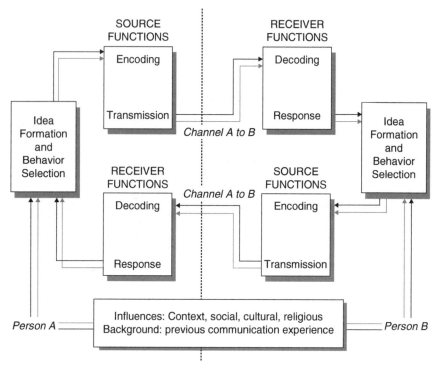

FIGURE 1.3 *Interpersonal communication model*

- *Receivers are active participants.* Because most receivers are active, this model shows that the receiver can be an active participant in the communication process. Receivers are assumed to react either verbally or nonverbally throughout the communication process. In contrast, some other models depict receivers as inactive, passive participants.
- *Each participant plays a dual role.* This model recognizes that each participant plays dual roles, acting as both a source and a receiver and that these roles often occur simultaneously.
- *Each participant gives and receives feedback.* The channel from person A to person B is the feedback channel for person B, and the channel from person B to person A is the feedback channel for person A. In other words, person A's message is person B's feedback, and person B's message is person A's feedback. Feedback occurs throughout the communication interaction. A and B both send and receive feedback simultaneously.
- *Participants communicate both verbally and nonverbally.* Communication involves more than just words. It involves the participant's

nonverbal communication, such as body, eye, and hand movements; body motions; facial expressions; vocalic inflections, and so on. Models that do not include the nonverbal component of communication limit communication to a verbal mode and, thus, do not account for much communication that takes place.

- *Participants are influenced by previous communication experiences.* This model of interpersonal communication assumes that what people say to one another is often affected by previous communication experiences. Often, how people interact is determined by the positive or negative experiences they have had with each other or other people in similar communication situations.

- *Participants are influenced by their background, experiences, and culture.* Often overlooked is the influence of a person's development of attitude, belief, and value systems that are typically a direct result of the educational, religious, and social background, combined experiences, and cultural backgrounds of the participant. Increasing research indicates that the cultural background of an individual has a definitive impact upon his interaction with others. For example, people reared and acculturated (learning and assimilating the cultural traits of a group of people) in Southern California versus upstate New York may have different attitudes, beliefs, and values because their cultural experiences and backgrounds are different. As a result, their communication styles, approaches, and orientations could differ.

- *Participants are influenced by their genetics.* Since the previous edition of this book was published in 1998, our understanding of the influence that an individual's genetic makeup has on his communication with others has grown extensively. We can now explain that when people are talking interpersonally, those interactions are influenced by both their cultural backgrounds and also their individual genetic makeup that influences their communicative patterns. For example, the hormone testosterone is highly associated with both physically and verbally aggressive behavior. Some people naturally produce more testosterone, which corresponds with an increase in physically and verbally aggressive interaction patterns. This one small hormone can have huge ramifications on how people ultimately interact with one another.

- *Communication participants are influenced by context.* This model of communication assumes that the context or situation in which communication takes place can influence the communication, participants, and outcomes. Issues such as surroundings, physical environmental cues, other people, and noise or lack of noise can all be factors in the communication process.

The above points illustrate the interactive, transactional nature of interpersonal communication. Collectively, these pointers allow us to view human communication from a more genuine, yet practical, approach. Today, this type of transactional, interactive model—incorporating all of the essential communication process elements—is accepted as most representative of interpersonal communication.

Now we'll review the seven essential components illustrated in this interpersonal model: source, message, channel, receivers, encoding, decoding, and feedback.

Source

The source is the person (or persons) who originates the message. The source usually performs three functions: (1) determines the meaning to be communicated; (2) encodes the meaning into a message that the receiver can understand; and (3) sends the message. Usually the source is the person sending the message as well as the originator of the message, but this may not always be the case. For example, news reporters are message senders, but are not necessarily the originators of the messages they transmit.

The source's functions sound simple, but this is not the case. If a source employs a language code to which the receiver cannot relate, the message might be misunderstood. This is a common problem. For example, the teacher (source) who uses terminology that the student (receiver) does not understand or identify with might not understand why the student fails an exam that uses the same language. This is one reason why representatives of an ethnic group may suggest that a standardized intelligence test does not accurately tap or evaluate the intelligence of all who take the test. The source of those tests are using the language to which they are accustomed, not necessarily the language used by the groups being tested. As you can see, the source's functions are critical to effective communication.

Message

The message is any verbal or nonverbal stimulus that might evoke meaning in the mind of the person receiving it. As an example of a nonverbal message, many of us try to communicate a certain image through clothing. Military and police uniforms communicate authority and have the effect of commanding respect. The student who comes to class with head shaven, chains, studded leather bracelets, and other leather apparel is communicating a different message. As discussed earlier, a message may be intentional or unintentional. Perhaps the student in leather is drawn naturally to such a style of dress or perhaps the student really wants to communicate that he is part of a subgroup.

People's number one fear is public speaking

Messages also might be interpreted unconsciously by their receivers. For example, if the door to a teacher's office is always closed between 9 and 10 a.m., students unconsciously learn to not interrupt the teacher during that time. Messages can also be very direct. One of our coauthors has a friend who will call on the phone or e-mail and blatantly say that he is having a "me day," which means he is not to be disturbed for any reason.

The message one sends will usually have components of both verbal and nonverbal communication; these two aspects of communication are inextricably linked. Finally, regardless of the intended meaning behind a message, it may or may not be interpreted by the receiver as was intended.

Channel

The channel is the means by which the message is conveyed from the source to the receiver. Channels consist of sound waves, light waves, the sense of touch or smell, and so on. Many times a message is sent through a combination of these channels. For example, when you tell someone you love him or her while hugging him or her, you have sent the same message through two different channels. In some situations, people can serve as channels. A message may be passed from a supervisor to a middle-level manager and then to the employees. If you remember the distorted messages that resulted from the childhood game of "telephone," when a message is whispered from person to person, then you can identify the biggest problem with a message passing through a "chain" of human channels. People tend to emphasize what is relevant to them, perhaps leaving out other vital information.

It is important to remember that the channels employed to transmit a message determine the outcome of the interaction. A source needs to determine what channel or channels will transmit the message. In human communication, we talk about three types of channels: verbal, nonverbal, and mediated. Verbal communication, as previously mentioned, involves the words we choose to use to communicate a specific idea. Nonverbal communication involves all the nonspoken messages that accompany or are used instead of a verbal message. As a quick caveat, please notice that we spell "nonverbal" human communication without a hyphen. We use this spelling of the word "nonverbal" to differentiate it from people who are non-verbal, or people who do not communicate using verbal messages for a range of different reasons. Last, mediated messages are messages transmitted using some form of mediating technology: newspapers, books, radio, television, cellphones, e-mail, the Internet, etc. . . . All three channels are important in human communication, and all three channels can create their own unique problems when utilized.

Receiver

The receiver is the person (or persons) who receives the message. The receiver might be an individual or a group. A message usually has an intended receiver, although there is no guarantee that the intended receiver will be reached; for example, if a television commercial for beer is run during Saturday morning cartoons, it may reach a mass audience, but it will certainly not reach the intended audience. (Advertisers spend untold time, energy, and money avoiding such costly mistakes.) There is also no way to ensure that the receiver will interpret the message as was intended (see the discussion under "encoding").

The receiver has three purposes in the interpersonal communication process: (1) receive the source's messages; (2) decode those messages into some meaning; and (3) respond to the messages.

Encoding

Encoding is the process of translating a preconceived idea into an appropriate message capable of being transmitted to a receiver. The encoding process consists of three parts: (1) creating the message; (2) adapting the message to the intended receiver; and (3) transmitting the message. Effective encoding depends on the source knowing what meaning a certain message will create in the receiver's mind. With words, gestures, colors, sounds, and so on, sources try to send messages that will create the intended meaning in the receiver's mind. It is important to remember that encoding is a receiver-oriented process, whether the receiver is one person or many.

Decoding

Conversely, decoding is a four-step process in which the receiver translates or interprets the message(s) he receives. In the first step of decoding the receiver *receives* the message, whether by hearing, seeing, or otherwise sensing it. (Remember that people receive messages usually through a combination of channels.) In the second step, the receiver determines what he thinks the source intended to communicate. This is commonly known as the interpretation stage. In the third step, the receiver *evaluates* the message in terms of its meaning and relationship to the receiver. Moreover, in the last step, the receiver *forms a response* to the source's message.

Feedback

The feedback component of the communication process is the receiver's response to the message after it has been seen or heard and then interpreted and evaluated. Feedback might be an overt, observable response, or it might be a covert, nonobservable internal response, or it may be both. For example, when a teacher asks a student to come to the front of the class to present a paper, the student's response might consist of moving from her or his seat to the front of the class (an overt response) while at the same time experiencing anxious feelings about speaking to the class (a covert response). The receiver's response to the source's message begins the cycle of the communication process, and soon the source is responding to the receiver's feedback in some manner. Now the source's thoughts and actions are being influenced by the receiver's feedback to the source's message.

Noise

Throughout the communication process, the *noise* element can intervene and disrupt the process. Noise can interfere in the transmission and/or the reception of the message. It can permeate the communication process at any time. For example, you might be transmitting through a faulty channel: Everyone has experienced the long-distance call during which static on the channel (noise) disrupts the communication exchange.

Noise might be either external or internal. Noise outside a classroom, for example (external noise), can affect the interaction between teacher and student. The student preparing to present a paper to the class might experience internal noise in the form of anxiety, which could easily interfere with effective transmission of the message. Daydreaming is another example of internal noise that can interfere in the communication process.

As we have seen, the components in the communication process are inter-related and depend on one another. The next section of this chapter reviews the various functions of the communication process.

Functions of the Communication Process

The functions of communication are the very reasons we communicate with others. We want others to like us, we want to understand the world around us, we want to influence others, we want to make effective deci-sions, and we want to be able to validate our decisions.

One of the most important functions of the communication process is known as *affinity-seeking*. This is the process of establishing and main-taining positive relationships. It is the ability to evoke positive feelings from others. The degree to which we experience social needs for affection and inclusion often manifests itself in our attempts to get other people to like and appreciate us. From a series of studies on affinity-seeking, researchers presented a list of the strategies people use to get others to "like" them. The strategies most commonly used were:

1. Conversational rule-keeping (following the rules of interacting, such as not interrupting);
2. Self-concept confirmation (making the other person feel good about themselves);
3. Eliciting other's disclosures (asking for information about the other, showing interest in what the other has to say);
4. Nonverbal immediacy (using nonverbal movements that indicate immediacy such as leaning close to the other, looking at the other person while talking, using positive facial expressions while the other is talking);
5. Self-inclusion (including other persons in your group and introduc-ing them to your friends, making them feel included);
6. Listening (being attentive when the other person is talking);
7. Facilitating enjoyment (making the relationship fun and enjoyable, at times being lighthearted, not always being serious, as serious can be boring); and
8. Altruism (doing nice things for the other person even if he or she doesn't ask, such as holding a door open for her or his, handing someone her or his coat, occasionally assisting her or his with work, and so on).

Affinity-seeking behaviors occur in a variety of communication situ-ations. For example, people use their communication skills to establish and maintain positive feelings in friendships, supervisor–subordinate relationships, teacher–student relationships, and most other relationships. Affinity-seeking behaviors usually result in increased liking and affinity, which in turn improves the communication between persons. Another function of the communication process is known as the *information and understanding function*. We are constantly sending and receiving information and interpreting the information. This function of communication enables us to grow, learn, and adapt ourselves and our messages to the world around us. As we process and understand information, we enable ourselves to react to the world around us and perhaps improve our responses to it. This text and other textbooks are devoted largely to this function, with a main goal of informing readers.

Influence is another important function of the communication process. This function is concerned with communicating in order to change people's ideas, beliefs, attitudes, and behavior. This function is usually considered successful only if one or more of these changes takes place. For example, if the receiver does not change his behavior or thinking, then the source has been unsuccessful. A teacher might keep students from cheating by physically standing over them and watching them while they take an exam, but this type of communication is not likely to effect a change in the students' overall philosophies about cheating—if the goal is to get students to be honest in every future situation, the communication is unsuccessful.

Being able to process and evaluate information and participate in the *decision-making function* of communication is a necessary skill. It is essential for all of us to make decisions, and often we need to communicate with others in order to do so; likewise, it is important for us to be able to assist others in making decisions about issues or events that will have an impact on their lives, as when parents want to be able to assist their children in making decisions.

The last function of the communication process is the *confirmation* of whether or not you made the correct decision about a new idea, practice, philosophy, or product. After we make a decision or a change, we either confirm or disconfirm our decision by seeking information to support our decision. For example, one of the authors of this text purchased a sporty car without first seeking details concerning its durability and reliability. Then, to confirm that he or she made a wise purchase decision, he or she spent several months talking with people who had similar kinds of cars, listening to the positive things they had to say (such as good gas mileage and durability). If we find information supporting our decision, then we are likely to stay with our original decision, although this does not prevent us from changing our minds in the future if information acquired later contradicts our original decision.

In summary, no matter how precise we are in our communication, there will always be variables that confound the communication process.

Human communication is an ongoing, dynamic, and change-oriented process. Much of this change and the meanings conveyed are manifested in the vast differences in which we communicate across contexts and with various individuals. By discussing the various communication models, types of communication, and components in the human communication process, we hope we have shed light on why the communication process requires skills, understanding, and a willingness to communicate in a competent manner. The next section focuses on common misconceptions about communication misconceptions that might produce ineffective communication between individuals.

Misconceptions about Communication

When we begin study in a new field, it is somewhat like meeting a new person. We might know (or think we know) something about that field. But after studying for a while, we realize some of our earlier conceptions were inaccurate or misleading. If we correct those assumptions, there will be no problem. If we don't, we may have problems in that field for years to come.

The field of communication is one about which most people know some things before they begin to study it formally. Unfortunately, most people in the general population have misconceptions about the communication process and how it works. These misconceptions often lead to ineffective communication; they also interfere with one's learning about communication. Let's look at ten of the most common conceptions about communication and consider why communication scholars believe they are misconceptions.

Misconception 1: Meanings are in the Words Themselves

This is probably the most common misconception about communication. Although people tend to assign meaning to the word, in fact meaning resides in the mind of the person sending the message and in the mind of the person receiving the message. The sender and the receiver may or may not have the same meaning in mind when they hear a word such as "love." Therefore, as communicators, we try to use a common code or language to communicate with others. However, a language is symbolic, and each of us interprets the symbols according to our personal and cultural background.

As an example of cross-cultural confusion inspired by meaning, several years ago the Pepsi Company had to cancel its Taiwan billboard campaign because its English slogan "Come Alive with the Pepsi Generation" was interpreted by the Taiwanese people as meaning "Pepsi will bring your ancestors back from the dead." Differing perceptions and interpretations within our own culture may be subtler, but the extent to which they can affect communication should never be underestimated. Thus, the accurate statement is that meaning is in the mind of the receiver. Both senders and receivers must keep this in mind when planning or interpreting a message.

Misconception 2: Interpersonal Communication is the Same as Intimate Communication

People in this culture assume that interpersonal and intimate communications are the same process and that communicating interpersonally means communicating in an intimate fashion. Intimate communication involves communication with another in which you discuss private information. In a lifetime, most people know only three or four people with whom they feel totally comfortable and to whom they can divulge intimate details and not worry about what the other will think or do with the information. Most of our communication is of an interpersonal nature, for example, asking a clerk in a store about new products, asking the time from a passerby on the street, conversing with a neighbor about the state of affairs in Russia. Very little communication on a daily basis is of a truly intimate nature. All intimate communication, however, is interpersonal.

The people with whom one person is intimate may not be the same people with whom another is intimate. For example, many people will disclose intimate information to their parents or one parent, while others will not. This doesn't mean those in the latter category don't have a close relationship with their parents; it simply means they don't communicate with their parents about intimate details. In marital dyads, sometimes one partner feels the other partner is not communicating as many intimate details as he should. Unfortunately, many long-term romantic partnerships are doomed to failure from the beginning because of the expectations one partner may have regarding such intimacy, since many people simply do not feel comfortable discussing the intimate details of their lives.

In the work environment, most interactions are of an interpersonal, not intimate, nature. Indeed, individuals in a workplace often feel uncomfortable if a colleague consistently discloses intimate bits of information about her or himself. People listening to this type of communication are likely to feel they should respond in a similar manner, which begins an irreversible and undesirable cycle. The work environment is probably not the place for intimate communication, but it is the place for interpersonal communication.

To clarify, how people become confused about the difference between intimate and interpersonal, let's discuss the three levels of communication (Miller & Steinberg, 1975): cultural, sociological, or psychological.

The *cultural level* of communication is when we communicate with one another based upon cultural expectations and norms. One way to learn about cultural norms and rituals is to communicate with people from various cultures. If we cannot physically communicate with people from cultures different from our own, we can at least read about their customs and make predictions about their ways of communication. Cultural communication can be successful if we understand and know the culture well, but our communication probably will be unsuccessful if our predictions do not match the cultural norms.

The *sociological level* of communication is determined by a person's association with groups or clubs. For example, if we wish to communicate with someone who is a member of the "group" we call high school students, and if we know further that this person is a member of an honors club and the debate club, we can make additional predictions about how to communicate with them. Groups are similar to cultures in that they have norms and rituals to which the members conform. Effective communication at the sociological level requires that we make accurate predictions of similarities among persons and we adapt our messages accordingly.

Monkey Business Images/Shutterstock.com

Talkative people are perceived as more competent, more attractive, more likely to be leaders, more powerful, and friendlier than less talkative people. Nevertheless, "the more communication" you have with others is not necessarily more effective communication with others.

The *psychological level* of communication involves adapting our communication to the unique attributes of the receiver. To do this, we must have direct, and often personal, contact with the receiver. McCroskey, Richmond, and Stewart (1986) and McCroskey and Richmond (1992) suggest this is the only level at which intimate communication can occur because intimate communication involves knowing each other through revealing private and personal information to one another. They further suggest that reaching the psychological level often is possible only after we have recognized and shared with each other our cultural and social similarities. It is for this reason that not all interpersonal communication is intimate—intimacy follows after we share, through other levels of interpersonal communication, our broader and more basic common views, beliefs, attitudes, and so on.

Thus, the accurate statement is that some interpersonal communication is intimate, but most is not. We rarely communicate with others on an intimate level, but we spend a lot of time communicating interpersonally.

Misconception 3: Communication is Solely a Verbal Process

Many people assume that the term "communication" refers exclusively to the process of talking and writing. In fact, a significant portion of our communication is nonverbal (gestures, facial expressions, and so on). The literature suggests that anywhere from 65% to 93% of the meanings stimulated in the communication process are produced by some nonverbal component. This information is not meant to suggest that verbal messages are less important than nonverbal, but rather illustrates the dual nature of communication. Nonverbal messages are most often associated with affect or emotion, while verbal messages are associated with ideational content (Richmond, McCroskey, & Payne, 1991).

Thus, the accurate statement is that communication is a verbal and a nonverbal process. Both components contribute to the effective encoding and decoding of a message.

Misconception 4: Telling is Communicating

People sometimes assume that telling someone something is effective communication. If this were true, people would only be told once how to do their jobs, how to make a bed, what to study for an exam, and how to drive a car. Communicating with someone involves much more than just telling. You must be able to adapt the message to the receiver and respond to the receiver's feedback. Individuals who operate with the belief that telling is communicating fail to recognize the active role of the receiver in the communication process. Those individuals are likely to be ineffective and insensitive communicators, unsuccessful at many functions of communication.

Thus, the more acceptable statement is that telling is only a part of communicating. People must be sensitive to the kinds of messages they are encoding, both verbal and nonverbal, and their potential impact on the receiver(s). Although the meanings that receivers may assign to our messages may not be the meanings we intended to "convey," we certainly have less reason to expect to achieve shared meaning by simply telling.

Misconception 5: Communication will Solve All Our Problems

We would all like to believe that simply by communicating with one another we will be able to resolve all conflict. We might think, for example, that if only the Iraqi government and the various cultures within the Iraqi countryside could get together and talk out their problems, then all internal conflicts would be resolved. In all likelihood, this is a fallacy since the various groups clearly disagree on values and issues and will probably never agree; in such a case communicating might actually do more harm than good. In fact, ineffective communication can create new problems or make problems worse than if no communication had been attempted. Effective communicators can distinguish between communication that will solve problems and that which will create problems; they know it is possible to "over-communicate" about an issue and resolve nothing. It is more realistic, then, to see communication as a catalyst that can create problems or help solve them.

Misconception 6: Communication is Always a Good Thing

If you go to any region in the United States and ask passersby if communication is a "good thing," the overwhelming majority will respond with a firm "Yes." As we have already noted, communication will not solve all problems and, in fact, might create some. Hence, it should be obvious that communication is not always a good thing. Communication is neither good nor bad. It is a tool. And, as with any other tool, we can abuse it or misuse it. If we use a hammer to pound in a nail, most would agree we have used the hammer correctly. If we use the hammer to break the glass out of our neighbor's window; however, most would agree we badly used the hammer. How a tool is used determines its effectiveness or ineffectiveness. The same is true for communication—how we use it determines its success. We are in control of communication just as we are in control of a hammer.

Misconception 7: The More Communication, the Better

More communication is not always better—it is the "quality" of the communication that is important. Certain norms in the U.S. culture, however, dictate that, unless it becomes extreme, the more a person talks the more positively he will be perceived by others. It is a sad fact, but a confirmed one, that in this culture talkative people are perceived as more competent, more attractive, more likely to be leaders, more powerful, and friendlier than less talkative people. Nevertheless, "the more communication, the better" is a misconception. For example, do we really need more e-mail, more text messages, and more spam sent to us today? We've almost gotten to a point of communication overkill. Furthermore, we would all agree that receiving more communication from a person we do not like and more stinging criticism from another is certainly not "better" than receiving less of these.

People equate quantity of talk with quality of talk, although it is not how much people communicate, but what they communicate that is essential. Nonetheless, there are people in our culture who rarely communicate with others and are perceived negatively for their lack of communication. An even bigger problem for some of these people when they do communicate is that their communication is ineffective or irrelevant. This is probably due to inexperience with the communication process. These poor communicators will be discussed more in later chapters.

Misconception 8: Communication Can Break Down

Someone having a problem communicating with another person tends to blame it on a communication breakdown. Communication is an ongoing, nonstatic process. Human communication does not break down or stop, although it might be ineffective. "Breakdown" is a nice way of suggesting that the communication itself was ineffective; almost as if the "tool" or the "process," not the sender or receiver, is to blame. In fact, the sender and receiver could simply be ineffective communicators. We need to remember that human communication does not break down like some technological machinery. It is simply ineffective. One cannot *not* communicate. Even if we stop talking we are still communicating because our nonverbal behaviors are sending cues to others. Many people like to use the "cold shoulder" or "silent treatment" on others when they don't want to verbalize their feelings. The recipient of the "silent treatment," however, is interpreting the message of silence; hence, communication has not stopped, it is simply being encoded differently.

Misconception 9: Communication is a Natural Human Ability

There are no natural born communicators, just as there are no natural born scientists, yet we are all born with the potential to be effective communicators. We learn and acquire our culture's communication skills, just as we learn and acquire our culture's social skills and manners. For example, did you just naturally learn not to belch in public? Or can you remember your parents at some point telling you not to belch in public? We learn social skills by observing, by modeling, by being reinforced for the appropriate behavior, and by trial and error. Some of us learn more and become better than others.

The same is true for communication. Most of us are born with this potential to learn communication; whether or not we acquire effective communication skills is up to our teachers and to us. Through careful instruction, personal observation, experience, and practice an individual can learn many of the communication skills needed to be a better communicator.

Misconception 10: Communication Competence Equals Communication Effectiveness

Competence cannot be equated with effectiveness. There are speakers the world over who are competent but not effective (the college professor who knows his subject thoroughly but bores students; the extremely competent supervisor who cannot communicate ideas to employees). Vladimir Putin is an example of a competent communicator who was also effective. Effective communication does not imply good messages, but Putin is effective at getting people to do what he wants. A speaker may also be a good, effective speaker without being "competent." For example, someone may deliver a moving and persuasive speech while not being informed about the issue.

If a person possesses a great amount of knowledge about a subject matter, he has a chance to be perceived as competent but may or may not be perceived as effective. Remember, a competent communicator could have a bad day and be perceived as ineffective, and an incompetent communicator could have a good day and be perceived as effective. Hence, communication competence cannot be equated with communication effectiveness, although competent communicators have the better chance of being perceived as effective. A basic reason that underlies misunderstanding in interpersonal relationships is that people have misconceptions about what communication is or is not and about how it functions. The purpose of this section was to pinpoint and assess 10 of the most common communication misconceptions. Chapter 2 examines factors that have profound bearing on a person's ability to communicate effectively and competently and on how we perceive the communication effectiveness and competence of others.

DISCUSSION QUESTIONS

1. Why will human communication continue to play a significant role in our lives, despite introducing new communication technology?
2. What is the definition of human communication?
3. What are the differences among accidental, expressive, and rhetorical communication? Give an example of each type of communication.
4. What are the drawbacks of the Shannon–Weaver communication model and the Berlo communication model?
5. Why is the basic interpersonal communication model more representative of the human communication process than the other two models presented?
6. What are the seven essential components needed in the human communication process? Give an example of each component.
7. Why is feedback so important in the human communication process?
8. Define noise. What are some examples of external and internal noise? What is its role in the human communication process?
9. Name the five primary functions of the communication process and give an example of each.
10. Describe each affinity-seeking function. Why is each function relevant to the human communication process?
11. Why do most people in the general population have misconceptions about the communication process and how it works?
12. What are the three basic levels of communication? Which one is considered to be the most intimate? Why?
13. Why is communication not solely a verbal process?
14. What component(s) are missing from the idea that "telling is communicating"?
15. Give an example of a situation where communication might not solve the problem, but actually make it worse.
16. Why is communication not always a good thing?
17. Why do people tend to equate quantity of talk with quality of talk? What is the problem with doing this?
18. If communication is an ongoing, nonstatic process, why do people use the ten-communication breakdown so often in relationships?
19. Why is no one born a natural communicator? What does it take to be an effective communicator?
20. What is the difference between communication competence and communication effectiveness? Which is the more desirable? Why?

ACTIVITIES

1. Review the five primary functions of the communication process. In a group, generate other goals a person could have for communicating. Give a rationalization for each new function generated.
2. Look especially at the affinity-seeking function of the communication process. In groups, list other ways that people try to get others to like them. Discuss why "being liked" is so important to our effective communication development.
3. List a situation in which you know you "accidentally" sent a message you did not intend to send to another. Give a detailed explanation of the situation.
4. Take the personalities Donald Trump, Barak Obama, Oprah Winfrey, and Alex Jones and discuss why each would be considered a competent and effective communicator.
5. Discuss a former interpersonal relationship you had with a teacher, employer, or friend and why the communication was effective or ineffective. What misconceptions did the participants overcome or fail to overcome?
6. In some situations, excessive communication can increase conflict instead of improving the situation. Describe such a situation.
7. Name a popular television show and discuss at least two of the misconceptions that have been ignored. How do the characters operate as if two of the misconceptions are true?
8. Discuss a situation in which you feel a person communicated information that was "too personal" or "too intimate" about himself to you, another person, or a group. How did you feel being the receiver of such information? How did others react to such information?

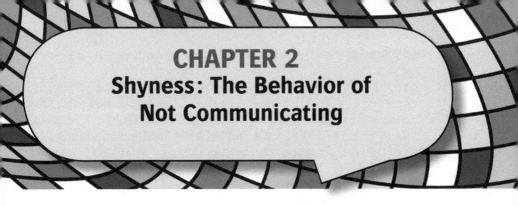

CHAPTER 2
Shyness: The Behavior of Not Communicating

In Chapter 1, we reviewed the functions of communication and how each function works and we examined the 10 most common misconceptions about communication and the impact each misconception has on the communication process. The remaining chapters discuss one of the most elusive phenomena regarding communication: how people differ regarding their desire for communication. Although some say that humans are social, this is only partially true. For a substantial portion of the population, being social and communicating with others is difficult, unrewarding, and sometimes impossible.

People with a high willingness to communicate attempt to communicate more often and work harder to make that communication effective than people with a low willingness to communicate, who make far fewer attempts and often aren't as effective at communicating. This second group of people is often unsuccessful at using and achieving the functions of communication. This lack of success means people unwilling to communicate might be less successful at affinity-seeking, gaining information and understanding, influencing others, making decisions, and confirming decisions than those people with a high willingness to communicate. In addition, the uncommunicative person might fare less well in social, work, and school relationships than those who like to communicate. The rest of this chapter reviews the major outcomes of noncommunication: shyness, quietness, or withdrawal behaviors in various situations.

Individual Differences in Communication

Much is made of the "uniqueness" of individual human beings. No two human beings are exactly alike, not even identical twins. The number of ways people can differ from one another probably is infinite, but one meaningful way in which we differ involves our patterns of communication. Many of our everyday references to people in our environment indicate our general awareness of such differences. We have all heard such comments as the following: "She is very quiet," "He seldom speaks up," "He never shuts up," "She has an opinion about everything and everyone,"

"He's a real gossip," "He always has something intelligent to say," "Getting an opinion out of her is like pulling teeth," "He's a real blowhard," and "They never talk, what's wrong with them?!" All of these comments have one thing in common: They refer to presumed habitual communication patterns of individuals that mark them as different from some (or many) other individuals. The comments differ from each other in that they refer to a variety of individual differences. The three most important types of differences fall into the categories of (1) effectiveness of communication, (2) amount of communication, and (3) desire for communication.

Effectiveness of Communication

All of us recognize that some people are far more effective communicators than are others. The successful salesperson, religious leader, politician, teacher, and manager are all obvious examples of effective communicators. Their opposite numbers are equally recognizable. There is a continuum that ranges from effective communicators to ineffective communicators with a large portion of the population falling in the middle. Those in the middle envy the effective communicators and thank their lucky stars they are not like the people at the opposite end of the continuum.

Amount of Communication

Although differences among people in terms of effectiveness are often easily recognizable, differences in the amount a person communicates (the number of times a person talks and the number of words said) are somewhat less obvious. You have probably noticed some of the following types of communicators:

1. The person who might be referred to as the "wallflower" at social gatherings and who, when approached, seems to want to get away;
2. The person in class who always has his hand raised to answer the question;
3. The person who always has a friend or relative speak for him or her;
4. The person who would rather stay at home or in his room playing on the computer rather than joining in social gatherings;
5. The person who avoids high-interaction areas in restaurants and clubs and would rather sit in the quiet corner;
6. The person who seems to be talking all the time, regardless of the situation;
7. The person who always has an answer for everything;
8. The teacher who assigns group work and oral reports so he or she doesn't have to talk;

9. The supervisor who rarely meets with subordinates or tries to help them solve work-related problems; and

10. A person who goes to her or his physician's office with a list of complaints but can't seem to ever talk about them.

From the above list, we can discern that there is a wide variety of communication behavior. Some of the differences can be accounted for by recognizing that as individuals we may talk more one day than another or more in one situation than another. Some of us talk more across virtually all situations, however, and some of us talk less across those same situations. In other words, we all fall somewhere on a continuum that goes from "talks a lot" to "seldom talks." Although many of us fall in the middle of the continuum, whether or not we talk is determined by the situation.

Desire for Communication

As suggested earlier, the desire to communicate differs from one person to another. Some people have a great willingness to communicate with other people, while some would be just as happy (or even happier) if they never had to communicate. Desire for communication can be found on a continuum that goes from great willingness to communicate with others to little willingness to communicate with others. At the extreme ends of the continuum, there are people who are willing to communicate a lot, and there are people who want to communicate as little as possible.

Desire is not as easy to tap or measure through observing behavior as is effectiveness or amount of communication. We can measure effectiveness by deciding in advance what effective communication is in a given context and determining how closely an individual comes to meeting that criterion. We can measure the amount by counting how long people talk and how many words they use. Desire is an internal state that can only be measured behaviorally by such indicants as withdrawing from communication with others, telling others you don't want to talk to them, avoiding potential communication situations, and generally acting shy. Such measures are quite imprecise. Consequently, desire can best be measured by self-report scales. We will consider some of these later. In conclusion, it is clear that individual differences in communication do exist, and they impact how we communicate and how others perceive us.

For example, the student who seldom interacts with peers, seldom asks questions in class, seldom goes to social functions, and rarely responds to the teacher's questions might be perceived negatively by peers as slow, unreliable, noncaring, or perhaps even as a trouble-maker. Hence, the individual differences in communication can determine how others will perceive and react to you. The next section of this chapter reviews the effects of individual differences regarding communication.

Effects of Individual Differences

In the United States, it is a well-known "fact" that there are a lot of people who talk too much. It is also a well-known "fact" that women talk a lot more than men and generally talk too much. These are two commonly accepted "facts" that have one thing in common: they are cultural truisms with no basis in fact. First, extensive research has been unable to discover any general differences between men and women in terms of either amount of talk or level of shyness. Some women talk more than others, so do some men. Some men talk less than others, so do some women. Second, extensive research indicates that the more a person talks, the more positively they are evaluated, other things being equal. What this indicates is that it is not an excessive amount of talking that causes people to have negative reactions, it is the quality of the content. For example, if someone is constantly talking about what a good student or what a good employee you are, you do not become upset with this amount of talk. If someone is constantly talking about what a good student or what a good employee he is, you may become upset with this amount of talk. Hence, it is the quality and not the quantity of talk that is important in determining other's reactions.

The grain of truth in the truism that there are a lot of people who talk too much is that we tend to notice and ascribe negative perceptions to people who talk a lot but have little worthwhile to say. The stereotype that women talk too much comes from the chauvinistic assumption that women are inferior and thus have little to contribute. We should also mention that research has shown that men engage in more talk than women. The key point to remember is that in U.S. culture, talk is highly valued. As a result, people in the culture have a shared stereotype that the person (man or woman) who talks more is worth more. Only when that stereotype is seriously violated by low quality of contribution are we willing to set the stereotypes aside and attribute the perception of "talks too much" to a person. But remember, in a chauvinistic environment it is much easier for a woman to violate the stereotype than it is for a man.

As a person's habitual level of talk increases, the person is perceived more positively. As a person's habitual level of talk decreases, the person is perceived less positively. Clearly, then, in U.S. culture, shyness is not a virtue. Most shy people recognize this. Only between 10% and 20% of these people consider their shyness not to be a problem; the rest consider their shyness a handicap.

Robert Kneschke/Shutterstock.com

Communication behavior-the person in class who always has her hand raised to answer the question.

Most research efforts in the areas of verbal behavior, willingness to communicate, communication avoidance, and shyness has focused on people in the United States. Virtually no extensive research has been conducted in most other cultures. However, enough research has been reported in some cultures to indicate that the stereotype of "the more talk the better" is also prevalent in England, Chile, Mexico, and New Zealand. Similarly, the proportion of shy people found in the United States has been found to be essentially the same as that in Germany, Mexico, and Taiwan. The proportion of shy people in Puerto Rico, Israel, and among American Jews, however, is substantially lower. In most instances, there have been no observed differences between men and women, although some exceptions have been noted. The exceptions include Japan (more men than women report being shy) and Israel, Mexico, and Germany (more women than men report being shy). We'll go into more detail about the impact of culture in Chapter 4.

It seems that the amount of talk generates comparable perceptions across most cultures—the more the better, the less the worse. The obvious conclusion one can draw from all of this is that all we have to do to be perceived more positively is to talk more. If other things are equal, that might be true, but things seldom are equal. As we have stressed, the element that interferes with this simplistic answer is quality of communication. Although it is true that people who talk a lot are perceived to produce higher-quality communication in many instances, there is also some truth to the old saying, "Keep quiet and let people think you are a fool, open your mouth and prove them right." The reason there is not a perfect correlation between the amount of talk and positive perceptions is that some very verbal people have little to say. The more they talk, the worse they are perceived.

In conclusion, for people who have a high willingness to communicate, but have little to say, reducing the talk level may increase positive perceptions. For people with a low willingness to communicate, the picture is crystal clear: Increased talk is the only path to more positive perceptions. It is not the quality of communication that is their problem, it is the amount.

The Nature of Shyness

Zimbardo (1977) and his associates proposed the following two questions to over 5,000 people:

- Do you presently consider yourself to be a shy person? ___ Yes ___ No.
- If you answered "No," was there ever a period in your life during which you considered yourself to be a shy person? ___ Yes ___ No.

The results are somewhat remarkable. They found that over 40% (2,000) of the people surveyed responded "Yes" to the first question and over 80% (4,000) responded "Yes" to one of the two questions. Projecting the results of this survey nationwide, the results indicate that two out of every five people you meet consider themselves to be shy, and two more believe they were shy at one time. Let's bring this closer to home. If there are 25 people at work, at least 10 of them think of themselves as being shy. One of them could be you or your supervisor.

Now that we know how many people in our country, on a percentage basis, consider themselves to be shy, what exactly is shyness? Defining shyness has not been an easy task for writers and scholars. Zimbardo himself has said, "shyness is a fuzzy concept," meaning that shyness is too vague a concept on which to pin a single concrete definition. Pilkonis, a former student of Zimbardo's, has offered a behavioral description of shy people. He suggests that shy people are "characterized by avoidance of social interaction, and when this is impossible, by inhibition, and an inability to respond in an engaging way; they are reluctant to talk to make eye contact, to gesture, and to smile" (Pilkonis, Heape, & Klein, 1980). Buss (1984) said, "shyness may be defined as discomfort, inhibition, and awkwardness in social situations, especially with people who are not familiar." He suggests that it is the absence of instrumental activity that identifies shyness. When someone is shy, he or she usually exhibits behaviors such as "withdrawal, reticence, and inhibition." He goes on to state that, "When we are shy, we tend to remain on the fringe of a conversational group, do not speak up, mumble minimal replies if addressed, and in general fail to hold up our end of the social interaction." He also suggests that the reaction might be so acute as to cause "shaking of the limbs, clumsy gestures, and stuttering" (p. 39). Do the above descriptions fit anyone you know? Shy people tend to be uncomfortable in the presence of others, to be easily frightened in social situations, and to talk significantly less than nonshy people. Shy people tend to be quiet people. Even if you are not a quiet person yourself, you certainly know people who are. People differ greatly from one another in their willingness to communicate, and by looking at behaviors we might be able to tell a shy person from a nonshy person. Before we discuss types of shyness, however, we need to look at causes of shyness.

The Causes of Shyness

As discussed earlier, the amount of communication people engage in differs greatly from one person to another: there are those people who talk constantly regardless of the situation and then there are those who seldom talk. Those in the latter category are the people who are usually labeled as shy, quiet, or unwilling to communicate. There are several reasons why a person might be shy, and the reasons vary from person to person. The following reasons seem to be the predominant ones: (1) heredity; (2) modeling; (3) childhood reinforcement; and (4) expectancy learning.

Heredity

You can look at your parents to see where you inherited such traits as height, tendency toward weight gain or slimness, eye color, and hair color. You may not be able to pinpoint where you received other qualities, however, such as your tendency to talk a lot or a little, your tendency to engage in social interaction or to avoid it. Until recently, heredity was discounted as a possible cause for differences in communication behavior and communication orientations. One only needed to point to major differences between siblings to suggest that heredity was not a credible explanation. In fact, no gene has been isolated that carries the communication trait. Scholars, however, are much less willing to disregard the role of heredity today than they once were, and some are even willing to argue that heredity may be the single most important predictor of communication orientations. Some people seem to be born talkers while others are simply quiet.

Recently, researchers in the area of social biology established that significant social traits can be measured in infants shortly after birth, and that infants differ sharply from each other on those traits. For example, infant "sociability," believed to be a predisposition directly related to adult sociability—the degree to which people reach out to other people and respond positively to contact with others—can be measured only a few weeks after birth. Other scholars have suggested that the extroversion/introversion orientation of an individual is an inherited trait and determines the orientation one has toward communication.

Research with identical twins and fraternal twins of the same sex reinforces this theoretical role of heredity. Identical twins are biologically identical, whereas fraternal twins are not. Thus, if differences between twins raised in the same environment are found to exist, biology can be discounted as a cause in one case but not the other. Actual research has indicated that biologically identical twins are much more similar in sociability than are fraternal twins. These research findings would be interesting if they were based on twin infants only, but they are even more interesting because research was conducted on a large sample of adult twins who had the opportunity to have many different and varied social experiences.

Researchers have argued for years over the impact of heredity on establishing individual differences in communication behavior and orientations. The issue is far from settled. We cannot discount the fact that heredity does give us predispositions toward communication, but predispositions can be changed by the surrounding environment. Thus, while heredity probably makes a contribution to the development of communication orientations like shyness or quietness, it is only part of the explanation.

Modeling

Nonverbal communication researchers posit that many of our acquired nonverbal behaviors come from modeling our parents, peers, and significant others. For example, little boys tend to walk much more like their fathers and other male models than like their mothers, while little girls tend to walk more like their mothers and other female models than their fathers. The modeling tendency is found in children as young as three to four years of age. Researchers suggest that parents see their children modeling their behavior and then reinforce it. As a result, the child continues the behavior.

Little research has been completed regarding the modeling of communication behaviors, but there does seem to be evidence that children observe the communication behaviors of their parents, peers, and significant others in their environment and attempt to emulate those individuals' communication. This certainly helps explain why children who grow up in southwest Texas have acquired the region's accent as opposed to a Bronx accent. Overall, modeling influences both general verbal and nonverbal behaviors.

If parents have a low willingness to communicate, then the child might learn this as the appropriate model and become less willing to communicate. If the same child enters grade school and finds that the majority of his elementary teachers are quiet types, then the model is reinforced, and the pattern possibly set for life. There is some research to suggest that children in lower grades who are exposed to teachers who have a low willingness to communicate might become less verbal themselves.

As suggested earlier, there is reason to believe that no one explanation is responsible for the development of communication orientations and behaviors. It is probable that modeling, and to an even greater degree modeling in conjunction with reinforcement, makes a large contribution.

Childhood Reinforcement

For years the theory of reinforcement has been the most popular explanation for behavior development and continuance. The basic premise of reinforcement is that behavior that is reinforced will increase and behavior that is not reinforced will decline. Hence if our communication is reinforced, then we will communicate more; if our communication is not reinforced, we will communicate less.

Of the three explanations we have examined so far, this is the only one that can claim to explain why children in the same family can be almost opposite one another in terms of their communication behaviors and orientations. One of our coauthors recently interacted with a student who came from a family with 16 siblings. She was the 16th sibling, and told our coauthor that she was more shy simply because it was hard for her to get heard above her siblings. Since parents, teachers, siblings, and peers reinforce each child differently, even within the same family, one child may be reinforced for communicating while another child is not.

Expectancy Learning

Much of the work in expectancy learning and its impact on communication orientations and behaviors is fairly recent, and research support for it is still forthcoming. The theory suggests that we seek to learn what consequences are likely to occur as a function of our behaviors (what to expect) and then try to adapt our behaviors in such a way that we increase positive outcomes and avoid negative outcomes. Therefore, if we learn that the more we talk, the more someone likes us and rewards us, the more likely we are to increase our talking behavior. Through the same process we learn what we should and should not say in specific situations. Thus, we learn what to expect under each of several options open to us: not to talk, to say A, to say B, to say C, and so on. In other words, a person makes her or his behavior choices because of the expectations of others.

Related to this explanation in a significant way is the phenomenon called "learned helplessness." In most areas of learning, over time we can develop solid expectations that are continually reinforced. In other areas, we are unable to do this. Research with laboratory animals indicates that when animals are confronted with such situations they become helpless and do nothing.

It is quite possible that in the area of communication some people confront situations like those of the laboratory animals and so do nothing. No matter what they say, they cannot learn to predict the reactions of other people in their environment; hence they do not communicate unless they absolutely have to. Much of this learned helplessness is created by an inconsistent reinforcement pattern. For example, at times a person might be reinforced for communicating A and at other times punished for communicating A, or a person is sometimes reinforced for talking and at other times is punished for talking.

Children and adults alike are often unable to sort out the situational differences that produce different responses from others even though their own behaviors are the same. Hence, they become helpless, and the only solution for them is to withdraw from communication. Such withdrawal is characteristic of the shy, quiet person, and such people often report feeling helpless in communicative situations. It is quite possible, then, that expectancy learning and reinforcement function together to produce the shy person. When expectations are learned, they result from consistent reinforcement patterns. When reinforcement patterns are inconsistent and unpredictable, expectancies are not learned, and helplessness followed by communication withdrawal is the consequence.

Types of Shy People

We have already noted that there are various explanations about why people are shy. There are several types of shy people, and each type is distinctly different from the other, but they all share the common characteristic of the shy person—they don't verbalize much or often.

Skill Deficient

It seems that everyone has at least one or two areas in which they are skill deficient. For example, some people will never be great athletes. In fact, they might never be even mediocre athletes and might always be poor athletes. There are also people who will never be good typists, mathematicians, cooks, and so on. All of the above have one thing in common: they never learned the skills necessary to be good at math, sports, and so on. Hence, because they know they are skill deficient, they have learned to avoid situations that show others they are skill deficient.

The same principle applies to communication. People who have poor skills in communicating may learn to avoid most communication situations. They may or may not make a conscious decision to avoid communicative situations—the behavior simply becomes a pattern. For example, a significant number of people in our society have communication disorders, such as stuttering, articulation disorders, and voice problems. Not all such people become low verbalizers, but many do. Similarly, people who do not speak English as their native language (e.g., the international student who learned English from a foreign English teacher) are very likely to become low verbalizers in situations that require speaking English. Likewise, many talkative Americans find they become low talkers when they travel in Europe among people who do not speak English.

In conclusion, many people become low verbalizers not because of a lack of desire to communicate, but because they lack the skills. If their skills could be improved, their communication attempts might increase.

Socially Introverted

One of the most heavily researched areas in the field of personality is that of extroversion/introversion. It has been demonstrated that people differ drastically in the degree to which they wish to be with other people. Some people have a high need and desire to be with other people (social extroverts), while others prefer to be alone most of the time (social introverts). The latter group will tend to be low verbalizers, not because of a lack of communication skills, but simply because they perceive little need for interaction.

Even though the social introvert is only one type of low verbalizer, it is interesting to note that people tend to perceive all low verbalizers as introverts and all high verbalizers as extroverts. This in itself causes us to misperceive people in many cases, most notably people in the public media whose job it is to be high verbalizers. Both Johnny Carson and Barbara Walters are seen by most TV viewers to be outgoing, extroverted people, and yet both have noted themselves as being somewhat shy and introverted.

To determine your level of introversion, complete the introversion scale (Appendix A). The norms for the scores on that scale also appear in that appendix.

Culturally Introverted

The norms presented in Appendix A for the introversion scale, as well as those for the other scales in the other appendices, are those based on college students in the United States. For most of these scales, the norms generated by other U.S. adults are nearly the same as those of college students. When we look at people from other parts of the world, however, we encounter some major differences.

For example, research completed in parts of Scandinavia and Asia (McCroskey & Richmond, 1990) shows that the populations of some

Some people are far more effective communicators than are others

countries are much more introverted than are the people of the United States. In some cultures, quietness is a virtue. Thus, factors that may lead an individual to be more verbal in one culture may not have a similar effect in another culture. Research indicates that Swedes (McCroskey, Burroughs, Daun, & Richmond, 1990) perceive themselves as much more competent communicators than Americans see themselves. Swedes, however, show they are less willing to communicate in most situations than are Americans. The Swedish culture is much more of an introverted culture than the culture in the United States, and simply seeing one's self as a competent communicator is not as likely to motivate a Swede to communicate as it might an American. Culture, then, may not only impact individual behavior, but it may also influence what people see as normative (hence appropriate) behavior in terms of communication in their society.

Socially Alienated

Most people in any society attempt to conform to the norms and values of that society. This behavior is considered a sign of the "well-adjusted" person. Because some individuals reject societal norms and values and make no attempt to conform, they become alienated from others and from society as a whole. One norm in most societies is that of a moderate to high amount of communication. The society values communication in its own right and also uses communication for the achievement of other goals and values. The individual who is socially alienated might reject the value of communication and become a low talker. In addition, the person might see little social merit in communication because the person is not interested in attaining the goals and values sought by other members of the society. Such people even put a negative value on communication because they see others employing it in ways they do not approve. Such orientations typically result in a low verbalization pattern for the individual.

Ethnically/Culturally Divergent

We often tend to confuse national citizenship and culture. We think and act as if everyone in a given nation or society shares the same culture. Although in some small countries this might be true, it is certainly not true in the United States. We have many ethnic groups and subcultural groups. Communication norms vary in these various groupings. For example, some tend to value silence more than talk.

But even though talk may be highly valued in ethnic or co-cultural groups, as people from the group interact on a larger scale with society, communication problems might arise. Although we might share a common language, we use the different dialects and accents of our subcultures to set us apart from other groups. Just moving from one part of the country to another (from the hills of Pennsylvania to the mountains of Montana) could present a problem. In each case, the person in the minority (whether he is Black, White, Hispanic, Latinx, Yankee, Southerner, or Texan) might not cope fully with the new communication demands he confronts and thus become less willing to talk.

The Communication Apprehensive

Communication apprehension (CA) is the fear or anxiety associated with either real or anticipated communication with another person or persons (McCroskey, 1984). By far one of the largest groups of quiet people is comprised of those who are communication apprehensive. Many people desire to communicate with others and recognize the importance of doing so but are impeded by their fear or anxiety. The person who has substandard communication skills or who is either ethnically or culturally divergent might also develop communication apprehension. Most communication apprehensive people have neither substandard skills nor are divergent from the general culture. They are simply people who are afraid to communicate.

It has been estimated that 20% of the general population (or one in five) suffers from communication apprehension. These results have been consistent across samples of subjects and from several subject populations (over 60,000 people surveyed). Communication apprehensive people tend to be low verbalizers. If one fears something, it is natural to avoid it or withdraw from it, and this is precisely what communication apprehensive people tend to do. Communication apprehension is an internal, cognitive state that is centered around the fear of communicating with others. Shyness is the behavior of withdrawing from communication or avoiding it, while communication apprehension is the fear of communicating, which causes shy behavior.

Not all quiet persons are communication apprehensive, but virtually all communication apprehensive persons are quiet. Communication apprehensive people differ from other quiet children in two important respects: they tend to have low self-esteem and a low level of willingness to communicate (WTC). It is important that this negative self-perception be carefully considered, because research suggests that such a perception is not justified. No substantial correlation has been observed between intelligence and level of CA. Thus, a person who is highly apprehensive could be just as bright (or ignorant) as any other person, but the negative self-image that accompanies CA is likely to be projected by the high CA person onto others. People who are highly apprehensive are often perceived negatively by others. Although negative self-image and high levels of CA are associated, it is important to note that neither one is the cause of the other. Rather, they both appear to be the product of particular reinforcement patterns that are experienced during preschool development and sustained after the person enters school. We further discuss communication apprehension in Chapter 3.

Willingness to Communicate

It is important to define the construct of willingness to communicate (WTC), which is a person's general attitude toward talking with others. This concept has emerged in communication literature within the last 20 years, and recent research suggests that WTC and CA are closely related (McCroskey, 1992). McCroskey states, "the construct is that of an orientation toward communication which we have referred to previously as a predisposition to approach or avoid communication. It specifically is posited to be associated with constructs relating to apprehension or anxiety about communication as well as constructs associated with a behavioral tendency regarding talking frequency" (p. 21).

An individual's level of CA probably is the single best predictor of a person's willingness to communicate. For example, the higher a person's communication apprehension level, the lower the person's willingness to communicate. WTC is a personality-based predisposition that determines the degree to which people talk in a variety of contexts. Whether a person is willing to communicate with another in a given interpersonal encounter (e.g., employee to boss) certainly is contingent upon the situational constraints of the encounter. Although WTC is situationally dependent, people usually exhibit regular WTC tendencies across situations. Communication apprehension is an internal, cognitive state that is centered around the fear of communicating; shyness is the behavior of withdrawing from communication or avoiding it; and willingness to communicate is the degree to which people are willing to initiate talk in a variety of contexts.

In summary, communication apprehension is what a person feels (he is fearful or anxious or simply scared; sometimes he is so anxious he simply can't talk at all—he is "scared speechless"). Willingness to communicate is one's general inclination toward talking, and shyness refers to the degree to which one refrains from actually talking. Subsequently, we are going to refer to some people as being "quiet." Although not everybody who is quiet is alike, the impact of their quietness tends to be generally about the same. So remember, not all quiet people are high communication apprehensives, but many are. Not all people who are quiet are unwilling to communicate, but many are. Not all people who are quiet are shy, but many are. Shy people are quiet, and it is their quietness that leads others to call them "shy."

We discuss communication apprehension (the feeling of being scared speechless) in Chapter 3. But before we do so, it is important to look at the contemporary measures of shyness.

Measures of Shyness

In the areas of shyness, communication apprehension, and avoidance, self-report measures are the most widely used approaches utilized to gage someone's communicative behaviors. There are other means of measuring, such as observing, watching videotapes, and coding live behaviors. These methods tend to be time-consuming, but when used in conjunction with the self-report, behavioral observation methods can be very useful.

The measures presented here are by no means all-inclusive, but they are contemporary and form a fairly substantial research base from which to predict shyness. As noted previously, shyness is considered to be the tendency to avoid communication and talk less. As discussed earlier in this chapter, the following measures are not specifically labeled measures of shyness, but this is what they appear to be measuring.

The simplest and best-known measure of shyness was developed by Zimbardo (1977). The two items on this measure are:

- Do you presently consider yourself to be a shy person? _____Yes _____No.

- If you answered "No," was there ever a period in your life during which you considered yourself to be a shy person? ____Yes ____No.
- A third item constructed by McCroskey is sometimes included to obtain additional information: If you answered "Yes" to the first question, do you consider your shyness a problem? In other words, would you rather not be shy? ____Yes ____ No.

McCroskey developed a Shyness Scale (McCroskey, Andersen, Richmond, & Wheeless in Appendix B). The Shyness Scale measure is a 14-step scale with good reliability and face validity, but the Zimbardo measure is still simpler and quicker to administer and, if only a crude measure is needed, is very useful.

More recently, McCroskey developed a WTC scale (Appendix C), the most direct measure available. This instrument measures a person's WTC in four contexts (public speaking, meetings, group discussions, and interpersonal conversation) with three types of receivers (strangers, acquaintances, and friends). Both the overall score and the subscores for the various contexts and types of receivers are highly reliable, and the face validity of the instrument is strong (McCroskey & Richmond, 1987; McCroskey, 1992). High willingness is associated with increased frequency and amount of communication, which in turn are associated with a variety of positive communication outcomes. Low willingness is associated with decreased frequency and amount of communication, which in turn are associated with a variety of negative communication outcomes.

In the communication field, the WTC scale is the best currently available measure of whether a person is willing to communicate with another person in an interpersonal encounter. The scale is convenient too, taking only a few minutes to complete. Because a person's willingness to communicate plays a central role in determining that individual's communicative impact on others, willingness to communicate deserves to receive a high degree of attention from communication scholars.

DISCUSSION QUESTIONS

1. What are the three most important individual differences in communication? Thoroughly discuss each one.
2. What has research determined are the general differences between men and women in terms of the amount of talk and level of shyness of each sex?
3. Why is talk so "highly valued" in U.S. culture? Are there other cultures where silence is a virtue? Please discuss.

4. How do Zimbardo and Pilkonis define shyness? Give some character-istics of shy people.
5. What are the major causes of shyness? From this list, which cause seems to contribute most to shyness? Why?
6. What does the research suggest about identical twins and fraternal twins in terms of communication development?
7. There are several types of shy people. Discuss five types.
8. What characteristic do all types of shy people share?
9. Communication literature makes distinctions among shyness, com-munication apprehension, and willingness to communicate. What are these distinctions? Why is it critical to know the difference among the constructs?
10. Although it's crude, what is the simplest, quickest measure of shy-ness? Why might one want to use this measure as opposed to others?

ACTIVITIES

1. Complete the Zimbardo Shyness Measure, the McCroskey Shyness Scale, and the Willingness to Communicate Scale. Compare your scores on each measure.
2. Talk with someone who is culturally or ethnically different from you. Note the differences in your speech and theirs. Attempt to find things in common with them, talk again, and see if communication improves.
3. Write a paragraph about someone you know who is shy, but use a fictitious name. Discuss her or his communication patterns and orientations.

CHAPTER 3
Scared Speechless: The Fear of Communication

Since 1970 more than any other single communication construct, communication apprehension (CA) has been a major concern of researchers and scholars. The reason for the intensive focus is because it permeates every facet of an individual's life—school, work, friendships, and so on . . . This chapter examines the types of CA, the measurement of CA, the personality correlates of CA, behaviors of quiet persons versus talkative persons, and the effects and causes of CA.

The Nature of Communication Apprehension

McCroskey (1970) originally viewed communication apprehension as "a broadly based anxiety related to oral communication" (p. 269). In later writings, CA came to be defined as "an individual's level of fear or anxiety associated with either real or anticipated communication with another person or persons" (McCroskey, 1977, p. 78). The term oral was included in the original definition since much of the early work on CA was founded upon work in the areas of stage fright and reticence. Because subsequent research did not focus strictly on talking, it was concluded that CA "encompasses all modes of communication" and should not be restricted to talking, although apprehension about talking is the more common form of CA (McCroskey, 1984).

In the 1970s, two groups of McCroskey's students extended research in the CA area. Daly and Miller's work (1975) in the area of writing apprehension and Andersen, Andersen, and Garrison's work (1978) in the area of singing apprehension spawned extension of the CA construct.

Writing Apprehension

Writing apprehension is the fear or anxiety associated with writing situations (Daly & Miller, 1975). Daly and Miller developed the Writing Apprehension Test (WAT), which is widely used in the field of English to measure a student's apprehension about writing. We created the Writing Anxiety Scale (WAS) as a short 10-item measure of this concept (Appendix D). A person's score on the WAT may range between 10 and 50. The higher the score, the more apprehension one feels about writing. Scores below 20 indicate a low level of writing anxiety. People with scores in this area are likely to enjoy writing and seek opportunities to write. The range of scores between 21 and 41 represent the "normal" range of apprehension about writing. For people in this range, some writing will create apprehension, while other writing will not. Scores above 41 indicate a high level of apprehension. People with such high scores are troubled about many kinds of writing and are likely to avoid it in most situations.

Daly and Miller's (1975) WAT has a moderate correlation (around .30) with the Personal Report of Communication Apprehension (PRCA), which focuses on oral communication apprehension. In other words, apprehensions about talking and writing are somewhat related, but it is quite possible for a person to be apprehensive about one form of communication but not apprehensive about the other. The PRCA will be discussed later in this chapter.

Singing Apprehension

Although the singing apprehension construct did not receive as much attention in the literature as did the CA research and the WAT research, it should still be noted as a concern of communication scholars in the area of CA. Andersen, Andersen, and Garrison (1978) developed the Test of Singing Apprehension (TOSA) to measure a person's fear or anxiety about singing. The TOSA was found to have a low correlation with the PRCA. Thus, apprehension about talking and about singing appear to be generally unrelated. To examine your own levels of singing anxiety, fill out the Singing Anxiety Test (SAT) located in Appendix E.

In sum, the CA construct was substantially broadened and redefined over the past decade. We now turn to the current conceptualization of CA.

The Biology of Fear

Our bodies are hardwired to react to fear-inducing objects and situations in a biological manner. In Figure 3.1, you can see the basic process our body goes through when we come in contact with something that causes us fear or anxiety. In this figure, we are assuming there is some kind of external stimulus that we cross, and our eyes are the first mechanism to trigger fear. However, there are definitely times when our other senses can trigger fear as well. With a fear-inducing situation, like public speaking, this process generally starts in the front part of our brain, the cerebral cortex, because that's where most cognitive thinking emerges. In the case of public speaking, just thinking about public speaking for some people is enough to trigger the biological fear response.

However, for most fears, the visual stimuli are transmitted through the visual thalamus to the visual cortex. When our brain sees "danger," it can transmit information directly to the amygdala. The visual cortex will also transmit information to the amygdala. The amygdala is an important feature in the human brain and processes both our memories and our emotional reactions to things. In a case where we fear something, our amygdala transmits a couple of interesting messages simultaneously. First, the amygdala tells the body to start pumping blood into our extremities (legs and arms). This extra pumping of blood will increase our heart rates and blood pressures. The amygdala also informs the muscles they need to contract and prepare for one of two possibilities: fight or flight (Siegel, 2005). Of course, this extra blood pumping to your extremities will increase the heat in those areas, which can lead to sweaty palms. Furthermore, the amygdala also tells the brain to stop other unnecessary phenomenon from occurring so that the body can focus on its desire to either fight the hazard or run away from the hazard. Your body may stop salivation production during the fight or flight, which could lead to a very dry mouth. Although these responses are great if you come across a bear in the wilderness, they may not be so great if your anxiety trigger is public speaking or speaking to another person interpersonally. For some people, the reaction their body has to communication is identical to the reaction their body would have coming across a bobcat in the wilderness. The body just experiences and reacts to fear-inducing objects or experiences, it doesn't differentiate among them.

In a recent study examining what happens neurologically between people who experience public speaking as fear and those who do not, the researchers found interesting differences in how the brain processes information while giving a speech. Tillfors et al. (2001) utilized a positron emission tomography (PET) scan to study how participants' brains looked while giving a public speech. The PET scan allows researchers to examine what parts of the brain are being triggered by measuring which parts of the brain are being activated. The researchers had two groups of participants. The first group consisted of people who had a fear of public speaking while the second group did not. In the group that did not have any fear of public speaking, the researchers found that those individuals relied primarily on the parts of their brains that handle cognitive thoughts and arguments (evolutionarily speaking the newer part of the human brain, or the cerebral cortex). On the other hand, individuals who had a fear of public speaking actually were triggering the part of their brain that recognizes dangers or hazards (evolutionarily speaking the older part of the human brain, also known as the animalistic part of the brain). In essence, people who fear public speaking are actually tapping into a part of their brain that is much older and much more primal than individuals who do not fear public speaking.

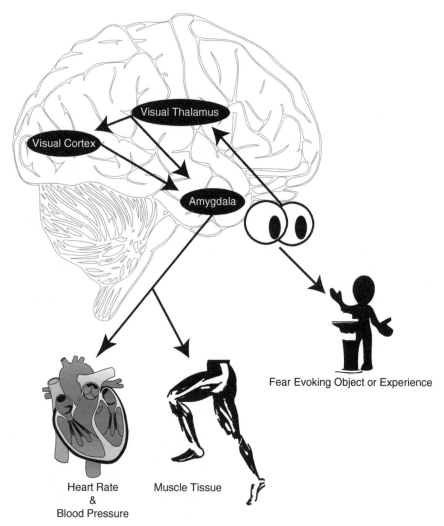

FIGURE 3.1 *Fear response process*

Types of Communication Apprehension

Based on research in the area of CA, it is useful to think of communication apprehension on a four-point continuum (see Figure 3.2). Starting at one end of the continuum and moving to the other the four points are:

1. Communication apprehension as a trait (traitlike CA);
2. Communication apprehension in a generalized context (context-based CA);

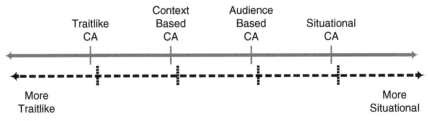

FIGURE 3.2 *Communication apprehension continuum*

3. Communication apprehension with a given audience across situations (audience-based CA); and
4. Communication apprehension with a given individual or group in a given situation (situational CA).

As McCroskey (1984) states, "this continuum can be viewed as ranging from the extreme trait pole to the extreme state pole, although neither the pure trait nor pure state probably exists as a meaningful consideration" (pp. 15–16).

Traitlike CA

The term "traitlike" was chosen because it indicates distinction between an actual trait (eye color, height, weight, and so on) and something that is traitlike. A true trait is "invariant" and cannot be changed. Of course, you can disguise your eye color by wearing tinted contact lenses, but you cannot change your true eye color permanently. Communication apprehension does not meet these criteria—that is, it is not a trait in the strictest sense of the term—but it is traitlike. Traitlike personality variables, such as CA, extroversion, and dogmatism are highly resistant to change, but this does not mean that they cannot be changed. Individuals, usually adults, might succeed at consciously changing aspects of their personalities, but such changes are usually accomplished in conjunction with some long-term effort on the part of the individual or a treatment program. Hence, traitlike CA is viewed as "a relatively enduring, personality-type orientation given mode of communication across a wide variety of contexts" (McCroskey, 1984, p. 16).

Most of the CA research in the 1970s concentrated on the study of traitlike CA. PRCA, WAT/WAS, and TOSA/SAT, discussed previously, measure a general predisposition, a traitlike personality-orientation. This assumes that a person's score on one of the measures will be similar across an extended period of time. In other words, traitlike personality orientations are expected to change little over time, unless there is some type of intervention program. Hence if you are generally traitlike communication apprehensive on Tuesday, you will probably be that way on Thursday of the following week and any Monday of the next year, unless you have treatment for reducing CA. During interviews with people who have high levels of communication apprehension, we have asked, "Do you ever feel less anxious?" The answer typically is "When I am with my family or with people I know very well; otherwise, I am usually anxious or scared about communicating with others." They often comment that the interview makes them very nervous, even though we are usually well acquainted with them before we ask such questions.

The Personal Report of Communication Apprehension-24 (PRCA-24: McCroskey, 1982) is the best available measure of traitlike communication apprehension (Appendix F). As with most personality-type measures, your PRCA-24 score can predict your behavior only if your score is extremely high or low. Such extreme scores suggest that your behavior is influenced as much, if not more, by your general feelings about communication than by the specific communication situation in which you find yourself. Either you are anxious or scared in virtually all communication situations or you are not. Scores may range from 24 to 120. Any score above 65 indicates that you are more generally apprehensive (scared) about communication than the average person. Scores above 80 indicate a very high level of traitlike CA (almost scared speechless). Scores below 50 indicate a very low level of CA (generally willing to talk). Extreme scores (either below 50 or above 80) are abnormal. This means that the degree of apprehension you experience may not be associated with a realistic response to a situation. For example, people with very low scores might not experience apprehension or anxiety in situations in which they should, and people with very high scores might experience apprehension or anxiety in situations where there is no rational reason for such behavior.

As noted earlier, about 20% of the population falls in each extreme category. It is important to clarify the meaning we are assigning to the terms low and high communication apprehension. People in the so called normal range of communication apprehension tend to respond very differently in various situations; one situation (a job interview) might prompt them to be highly anxious while another situation (answering a question in class) might result in no anxiety or tension at all. The "low" and the "high" communication apprehensive, however, tends to respond to virtually all oral communication situations in the same way. The low CA will usually be willing to talk and not be scared to communicate. The high CA will usually be unwilling to talk, remain quiet, and be scared speechless most of the time. In summary, traitlike CA is an enduring orientation about communication and usually doesn't change unless there is some form of intervention or behavior modification.

Context-Based CA

This type of CA relates to people who are fearful or anxious about communicating in one type of context, while having no fear or anxiety in other contexts. The most common form of this is the fear of public speaking or stage fright.

Context-based CA is viewed as a "relatively enduring, personality-type orientation toward communication in a given type of context" (McCroskey, 1984, p. 16). This type of CA relates to generalized situations. Examples of such situations, besides public speaking, include going on job interviews, meeting new people, and the like. The Personal Report of Public Speaking Anxiety (PRPSA: McCroskey, 1970) will determine your fear about public speaking (Appendix G). Your score on the PRPSA can range between 34 and 170.

For people with scores between 34 and 84 on the PRPSA, very few public speaking situations would produce anxiety. Scores between 85 and 92 indicate a moderately low level of anxiety about public speaking. Although some public speaking situations would be likely to arouse anxiety in people with such scores, most situations would not be anxiety arousing. Scores between 93 and 110 indicate moderate anxiety in most public speaking situations, but the level of anxiety is not likely to be so severe that the individual won't be able to cope with it, eventually becoming a successful speaker. Scores that range between 111 and 119 suggest a moderately high level of anxiety about public speaking. People with such scores will tend to avoid public speaking because it usually arouses a fairly high level of anxiety. Although some public speaking situations may not cause too much of a problem, most will be problematic. Scores between 120 and 170 indicate a very high level of anxiety about public speaking. People with scores in this range have very high anxiety in most, if not all, public speaking situations and are likely to go to considerable lengths to avoid them. It is unlikely that they can become successful public speakers unless they overcome or significantly reduce their anxiety.

When we discuss oral communication apprehension and the PRCA-24, we note that the "normal" range of scores includes only moderate levels of CA. The picture is quite different when we look at anxiety about public speaking. Of the several thousand college students who have completed the PRPSA, the following percentages have been found in the five categories: low anxiety, 5%; moderately low anxiety, 5%; moderate anxiety, 20%; moderately high anxiety, 30%; and high anxiety, 40%. Thus, the "normal" range for public speaking is in the moderate to high categories, since that is where most people's scores fall.

What this suggests, then, is that it is "normal" to experience a fairly high degree of anxiety about public speaking. Most people do. If you are highly anxious about public speaking, then you are "normal."

Although there is no necessary relationship between trait communication apprehension level and level of communication apprehension concerning any particular generalized context, it is much more likely that a person who is high in traitlike communication apprehension will have high communication apprehension in more generalized contexts. The reverse is true for the person with low trait communication apprehension.

Here, of particular importance is the proportion of people who experience high communication apprehension in given situations. Although only 20% of the population experiences high traitlike communication apprehension, estimates run as high as 80% of the population for generalized context communication apprehension—over 70% for public speaking context alone. Thus, while such communication apprehension is likely to make one uncomfortable and interfere with communication, it is normal for a person to experience high communication apprehension (to be scared) in at least one situation.

McCroskey and Richmond (1980, 1982) developed measures of communication apprehension in generalized contexts (Appendix H). To obtain a rough idea about your level of communication apprehension in generalized contexts, complete the five measures in Appendix H. By comparing your score on each of the other four scales with your general score on the scale, you can identify what kinds of situations—talking in groups, meetings, interpersonal conversations, or giving speeches—cause you to be more or less apprehensive. Any score above 30 indicates some communication apprehension; scores above 35 indicate a comparatively high level of communication apprehension.

Audience-Based CA

Audience-based CA is concerned with a person's reactions to communicating with a given individual or group of individuals across time. For example, some individuals and groups might cause a person to be highly apprehensive, while other individuals or groups do not produce anxiety. This type of CA is situation specific and might not be the same from person to person. Almost 95% of the population, however, reports being scared about communicating with a person or group at some point in life. The target that produces this fear might be a boss, father, teacher, colleague at work, or virtually anyone else in a person's environment. It is quite normal to be apprehensive when communicating with certain individuals or groups.

Audience-based CA is viewed as "a relatively enduring orientation toward communication with a given person or group of people" (McCroskey, 1984, p. 17). This type of CA is not seen as personality-based, but as a response to situational constraints generated by the other person or group. Although it is not possible to predict which people will make high trait communication apprehensives most uncomfortable or low trait communication apprehensives most uncomfortable, we do know that the high trait apprehensives (those afraid of most communication situations) will have apprehension aroused in them by more people than will the low trait apprehensives. Once again, the trait of high communication apprehension is reflected in an increased probability of fear or anxiety in almost all situations. This type of CA is produced by the situational constraints more than by the personality of the individual. Hence length of acquaintance should be considered. Richmond (1978) found that while personality orientations should be expected to be somewhat predictive in the early stages of acquaintance of CA, in later stages of acquaintance the situational constraints predict more of the apprehension experienced by the individual.

Much less attention has been paid to the measurement of audience-based CA than traitlike CA. However, Spielberger (1966) developed a state anxiety measure later modified by Richmond (1978). The recently developed measure of this type of CA is known as the Situational Communication Apprehension Measure (SCAM; McCroskey and Richmond, 1982). Your score on this measure may range between 20 and 140.

The SCAM is designed to measure the apprehension you feel while participating in a specific communication situation or talking with a specific audience. As a result, it can be used to measure your apprehension about any situation or audience, such as talking with your supervisor or your parents, giving an oral report in class, going on a job interview, calling someone for a date, or simply as answering the phone to talk with a stranger. Using the SCAM measure (see Appendix I), we ask you to complete the scale with regard to how you felt in your last interaction with someone who was in a supervisory position over you (a teacher if you are a student, your principal if you are a teacher, and so on). We chose this situation arbitrarily; any other situation could illustrate the SCAM as well. If you are apprehensive about asking someone for a date, use this and complete the measure.

Scores on the SCAM between 20 and 50 indicate very low apprehension about the given communication situation. This is the amount of apprehension a typical person might feel while talking with a close friend. Scores between 70 and 90 represent a moderate amount of apprehension. A score in this range would suggest some discomfort, but not enough for a person to avoid the interaction. Scores from 110 to 140 indicate a very high level of apprehension. It is quite likely that if a person feels this extreme apprehension in a situation, that person will try to avoid the same situation in the future. If the situation cannot be avoided, that person might be a low talker (or very quiet) in this instance.

There is no way to estimate what is "normal" on the SCAM since it is clearly "normal" to respond differently in similar situations. If you were to complete the scale on several different audiences, you would see quite a variety in your scores. Of course, because it measures extremes, people who have high PRCA-24 scores are likely to have high SCAM scores in more situations than would other people, and the reverse would be true for people with low PRCA-24 scores.

Situational CA

At the far end of our continuum is communication apprehension that is experienced only with a given individual or group in a single situation. Virtually 100% of us experience this form of communication apprehension at one time or another. For example, when your teacher tells you that he suspects you of cheating; when your boss tells you he or she suspects you of "borrowing" company equipment; when with 5 minutes' notice you are expected to give a 20-minute group presentation on a topic you know very little about; or when you have to go to court to testify in a trial. Situational CA is viewed as "a transitory orientation toward communication with a given person or group of people." It is not viewed as personality based, but rather "as a response to the situational constraints generated by the other person or group" (McCroskey, 1984, p. 18). This type of CA will fluctuate as constraints introduced by the other person or group fluctuate. Even though people with high traitlike CA and high context-based CA would be expected to experience high situational CA, knowledge of levels of neither of these should be highly predictive of which situations will produce the high CA. Audience-based CA, however, should be moderately high related to situational CA because both are concerned with group anxiety.

Situational CA has received little attention in terms of measurement compared with the other types, but the SCAM is often used to satisfactorily measure situational CA (McCroskey, 1984; McCroskey and Richmond, 1982). To summarize, traitlike CA cuts across time, receiver, and situation. This is what would be expected with a personality orientation such as traitlike CA. Context-based CA is associated with a single type of communication context cutting across receiver and time. Audience-based CA is seen as apprehension that is associated with a single receiver or group of receivers cutting across context and time. Situational CA is apprehension specific to a given context with a given receiver at a given time.

Pathological Behavior

This is not necessarily a type of CA, but indicative of a unique person who either experiences CA when he or she should not or never experiences

CA even when he or she should. CA has an impact on every individual to a greater or lesser extent, but when someone behaves abnormally to threatening situations (such as not withdrawing), he or she is considered pathological.

Pathological behavior also encompasses such situations as when a person talks excessively at inappropriate times, regardless of the circumstances surrounding the situation. Even though this person is an obvious low apprehensive (not afraid of speaking out) such behavior is still pathological in the sense that the individual doesn't know how to gauge appropriate communication behavior. This definition might sound like it defines many of your friends, but pathological behavior is extreme. Several years ago, we became acquainted with a university faculty member who never ceased talking, even when the dean of the college told him it was time to be quiet. Eventually, this person was asked to leave the university, largely due to his deviant, pathological behavior. He was an authority on all things regardless of their nature, and his colleagues simply couldn't work with him. Hence pathological CA can take the form of a person who talks when he shouldn't (the low apprehensive who is never afraid to say anything at any time) or a person who won't talk when he should (the high apprehensive who is afraid to talk even when the situation is nonthreatening). As stated earlier, some groups of people might appear pathological but are not. For example, if you ever attended a conference for top-notch sales persons, you know they often talk constantly. This is their orientation: the more you talk, the more you sell. Hence this is normal communication behavior for their group. In addition, keep in mind that some cultures value quietness more than talk. Although people in these cultures may seem excessively quiet to us, they are nonetheless displaying normal communication behavior.

We should be clear from the discussion of the four types of CA that a person's level of traitlike CA is very much a part of that person's overall personality. Our next section reviews the personality correlates of traitlike CA (the persons who are scared speechless).

Causes of Communication Apprehension

Now that we have discussed the effects of quietness, we can turn our attention to the causes. The following is a discussion of the causes of traitlike CA and the causes of state/situational CA.

Causes of Traitlike Communication Apprehension

As with shyness, heredity appears to be a meaningful contributor to traitlike CA (McCroskey & Richmond, 1978, 1980, 1982). Children are born with certain personality predispositions, such as sociability. How this sociability is treated by parents can often determine whether or not a child will develop high CA. The predisposition exists, but environment also plays a major role. How and when the child is reinforced for communication will determine to some extent whether the child will develop high CA or an inclination toward quietness. If a child is reinforced for communicating, he or she will probably communicate more. However, if the child is punished for communication or the communication is ignored, he or she might communicate less. This simple reinforcement theory alone, however, does not account for all development.

As suggested in Chapter 2, modeling can play a role in the development of shyness and communication apprehension. Hutchinson and Neuliep (1993) found that a father's apprehension level and parental modeling were significantly related to apprehension in children. They also found that peer modeling and a mother's apprehension level were not related to communication apprehension in children. Although the results are not always conclusive, it is clear that modeling has the potential to contribute to traitlike communication apprehension.

Many children receive mixed cues or inconsistent punishment and reward for communication. As a result, they cannot predict what or when to communicate. They learn to be helpless because of the inconsistent reinforcement patterns of their parents, teachers, peers, and so on. There is no predictability on how or what to communicate, so they avoid communicating with others. For example, little Johnny is allowed to talk during

The person with a high degree of general anxiety is uneasy and worried virtually all the time, whether or not there is good reason for such concern.

the TV news one night at the dinner table, the next night he is punished for it, two nights later he is allowed to talk again. If this type of inconsistent reinforcement pattern continues in other communication facets of Johnny's life, it is likely he will learn the only way to win is to withdraw. He has learned to be apprehensive about communication.

Furthermore, scholars have been examining the impact that one's genetic makeup may have on her or his level of communication apprehension. As discussed earlier in this chapter, the idea that fear may be biologically triggered and evolutionarily transmitted has been tossed around since the 1970s. The first real discussion of communication apprehension possibly being a result of biological processes occurred in the seminal article by Beatty, McCroskey, and Heisel in 1998. Beatty et al. (1998) argued that for too long researchers have only been investigating communication apprehension from a social learning perspective. Social learning basically theorizes that how we behave and think are a result of the experiences we have had in life. In this case, people who have trait levels of CA do so because of experiences that instilled high levels of CA. A temperamental perspective, as advocated by Beatty et al. (1998), argues that people who have trait-levels of communication apprehension may be predisposed to those high levels as a result of their genetic makeup.

The temperamental approach to understanding human behavior, as advocated by Hans Eysenck (1998), theorizes that there are three supertraits: extraversion, neuroticism, and psychoticism. Extraversion is the tendency to be outgoing and sociable. Neuroticism is the tendency to fluctuate between mania (really happy) and depression (really sad). Psychoticism is the tendency to be antisocial and believe that society's rules and norms do not apply to you. Eysenck (1998) believes that our genetics cause each of us to exhibit different levels of extraversion, neuroticism, and psychoticism. Then based on the combination of the levels of the three supertraits, we exhibit specific human behaviors. In the case of communication apprehension, Beatty et al. (1998) found that individuals who exhibited low levels of extraversion and high levels of neuroticism were considerably more likely to be communicatively apprehensive. For CA, the supertrait psychoticism did not play a part in the equation.

Based on this research, Beatty et al. (1998) coined the term "communibiology" to examine the new field of communication research examining the biological underpinnings of some communication behaviors. Although Beatty et al. (1998) and then Beatty, McCroskey, and Valencic (2001) argue that biology helps us to understand human behavior, all parties are quick to acknowledge that biology is only a part of the picture. Although biology may help us to understand people who have trait levels of CA, biology is less likely help us to understand the other levels of CA.

Causes of Situational Communication Apprehension

The causes of situational or state CA are numerous and can vary from one person to another or from one situation to another. Here, we discuss only the primary causes of situational CA, using the major causes of apprehension as outlined by Buss (1980): novelty, formality, subordinate status, conspicuousness, unfamiliarity, dissimilarity, and degree of attention from others.

The *novel* situation will usually cause an individual some anxiety because he does not know how to react or communicate. For example, going for a job interview might be novel for a lot of people, and they will probably be quite nervous. But after they have been to a few job interviews, they will be less nervous and know what to predict. It is the uncertainty or unpredictability of the situation that creates the state anxiety.

Formal situations increase anxiety because there is very little latitude for deviation from the norm. Hence a person's state CA will increase because he does not want to communicate inappropriately. You have all experienced that formal situation in which you know if you communicate inappropriately you will be publicly embarrassed.

Subordinate status occurs when a person holds "high status" over another. An example of this is when an important public official (the president of the United States) meets with a citizen to discuss issues. The citizen might experience situational shyness. Buss states, "a common outcome is gaze aversion, shrinking from close contact, and an inability to converse normally—in brief, shyness" (p. 188).

Would you like to stand naked on a crowded street corner? The answer is probably no. Almost nothing makes one more nervous and anxious than feeling *conspicuous*. Being a new person in class makes one conspicuous. Being the person singled out to answer a question in an important meeting makes one conspicuous. As we feel more conspicuous, our anxiety level tends to escalate.

Being unfamiliar with the norms in a culture can make one uncomfortable. For example, one of the authors travels to other countries and always comments on how uncomfortable he feels when trying to communicate in a different culture because he is not familiar with their norms for communication. If you feel uncomfortable with another, anxiety increases. As unfamiliarity increases so does state apprehension.

Dissimilarity is an extension of unfamiliarity. The more dissimilar we are to others, the more difficulty we have communicating with them. As dissimilarity increases so does anxiety.

Excessive attention can create situational anxiety. Most of us like attention from others. Few of us, however, want to be the center of focus of attention all the time because it makes us uncomfortable and uneasy. We like a moderate amount of attention. If attention is too high, our anxiety increases. Excessive attention differs slightly from conspicuousness in that excessive attention is being put "on the spot" or being given an inordinate amount of attention. Excessive attention could contribute to our feelings of conspicuousness, but excessive attention is not the same feeling as conspicuousness.

We have discussed some of the common causes of state apprehension. Daly and Hailey (1980) introduced two more: *degree of evaluation* and *prior history*. If one feels he or she is constantly being evaluated, then her or his communication anxiety will increase. For example, some students who normally do not experience anxiety while speaking before other people become so during a public-speaking course because of the added pressure of a teacher sitting in the back of the room grading them. This extra emphasis on being evaluated is what ultimately triggers their anxiety. In addition, if one has a prior history of failure with a certain individual or group, the anxiety will increase when confronting that individual or group.

In conclusion, situational communication apprehension or anxiety might be caused by a number of elements, but the elements that cause state anxiety or one may not cause it for another. We know that in everyday life, negative reactions from others and novel, conspicuousness, and unfamiliar situations can make us anxious about communicating. We have to learn methods of coping with various communication contexts that make us nervous. Chapter 7 explores various methods for helping people reduce communication anxiety.

Effects of Communication Apprehension

The primary effects of apprehension can be divided into two categories: (1) those that are experienced internally and (2) those external effects that others can observe. The external effects are highly related to one's willingness to communicate or one's level of quietness.

Internal Effects

Communication apprehension is a cognitive response to communication that arouses one internally. McCroskey (1984) states that, "the only effect of CA that is predicted to be universal across both individuals and types of CA is an internally experienced feeling of discomfort" (p. 33). The lower the level of CA, the less the feeling of discomfort. People with low CA will still have physiological arousal about communicating, but their internal feeling is one of excitement or pleasure, not one of discomfort such as the high CA experiences. The internal feeling the high CA individual experiences is one of discomfort, fright, being unable to cope, being inadequate, and possibly being dumb. Common physiological effects associated with this internal fear might be rapid beating of the heart, queasy stomach, increased perspiration, some shakiness, and dry mouth.

External Effects

There are three common behavioral responses to the fear of communicating: communication avoidance, communication withdrawal, and communication disruption. A rare, but worth mentioning, behavioral response is "over-communication." Our discussions have touched on all of these, but we will summarize here.

Avoidance: If a person is fearful of someone or something, a common response is to avoid that person or the situation. This is often the case for people who are not willing to communicate or afraid to communicate. They choose (either intentionally or unintentionally) to avoid communication with others whenever possible. They choose to avoid situations that might require them to communicate. For example, they will avoid classes that have required speeches and teachers who call upon students to answer questions in class. They will avoid occupations that require a high level of communication.

Withdrawal: Since avoidance is not always possible, the low WTC might withdraw from the communication situation. Often the low WTC will find herself or himself in a situation that requires communication. Hence, he or she will withdraw by not answering questions or giving minimal communication. This is common in the classroom. The low WTC student will avoid communication with her or his teacher when possible. When this is not possible, the student will often not respond to a teacher's question or will give minimal or even wrong responses. This almost always guarantees that the teacher will leave the low WTC student alone, but the student runs the risk of the teacher having a bad impression because of this type of withdrawal behavior.

Disruption: Communication disruption occurs when the person has disfluencies in verbal speech or unusual nonverbal behaviors. For example, it might seem as if he or she has a stutter or can't remember what he or she was going to say, or he or she might get a twitch in her or his cheek or bite her or his nails or look anywhere but at the receiver. All of the above could also be responses from a person who has poor communication skills. Hence this behavior is not as accurate a predictor of WTC as the other two.

Over-communication: Over-communication is rare for the quiet individual, but there may be cases in which a person extremely high in CA conceals her or his fear by talking all the time. Again, this is a rare, unusual response.

The first two effects discussed here, avoidance and withdrawal, involve the flight syndrome—the quiet person decides to take flight from communication. In over-communication, the quiet person fights back by talking all he or she can, regardless of whether he or she has a lot to say. This communication usually is ineffective, and often this person is seen as an unskilled communicator.

In conclusion, the quiet individual experiences internal and external effects, both of which are debilitating. We now need to look at the causes of traitlike and state communication apprehension.

Personality Correlates of Apprehension

Communication apprehension is very much a part of a person's overall personality. Although no two human beings are exactly alike, if they possess similar traits and personality characteristics one can predict how they might respond in different situations: This section examines the personality patterns of people with high levels (talkative persons) and low levels (quiet persons) of traitlike CA. Sorenson and McCroskey (1977) and McCroskey, Richmond, Daly, and Falcione (1977) completed much of this work. This will assist us in understanding how each type of person approaches his environment and interacts with others.

General Anxiety

General anxiety is characterized by uneasiness and worry that spans many situations. The person with a high degree of general anxiety is uneasy and worried virtually all the time, whether or not there is good reason for such concern. This person is likely to be restless, impatient, and tense.

General anxiety is often confused with communication apprehension. It is easy to understand why this confusion occurs, since people with either high communication apprehension or high general anxiety are likely to exhibit some of the same behaviors. They may fidget, repeat themselves, get dry mouths or upset stomachs, and so on. The key difference is that these characteristics are common to persons with high general anxiety both in communication situations and in other situations, whereas for high communication apprehensives they only occur in communication situations.

Although these two aspects of personality are not the same thing, this does not mean they are not related. People with high levels of general anxiety are more likely to be high communication apprehensives, and vice versa. Similarly, people with low levels of communication apprehension are less likely to have a high level of general anxiety. It is important to remember, however, that just because a person has a high or low level of communication apprehension, it does not necessarily follow that the person has a matching level of general anxiety.

Tolerance for Ambiguity

Some people have a personality that allows them to function in a communication environment in which there exists a lot of uncertainty. Other people have little or no tolerance for uncertain situations. This personality variable is known as "tolerance for ambiguity."

People with a low tolerance for ambiguity are likely to have higher levels of communication apprehension. Similarly, people with high levels of tolerance for ambiguity are likely to have lower levels of communication apprehension. When confronted with an ambiguous situation, these two types of people are likely to behave differently: Since such situations increase demands for communication, the high communication apprehensive is likely to withdraw, whereas the low communication apprehensive is likely to increase communication. For example, if a couple is in an ambiguous relationship, as communication apprehension increases, tolerance for ambiguous communication decreases and the probability of withdrawal increases.

Self-Control

Self-control dictates how much control a person has over his own emotions. Degree of self-control and communication apprehension are negatively related; as communication apprehension increases, self-control tends to decrease. As might be expected, people high in self-control tend to be calmer, more composed, more in control in general, and less afraid of communicating. People who are low in self-control are more likely to be high communication apprehensives. They are afraid to talk and communicate because they are insecure and lack control over their emotional states. They may withdraw from communication so that they do not lose control over their emotions and say things they do not mean.

Adventurousness

A person with an adventurous personality is one who enjoys new experiences and tends to become bored with routine or repetitive matters. Such people like to experience new things, people, places, and ideas. They tend to be more sociable and outgoing and have a lot of variability in their emotional responses. People low in adventurousness, on the other hand, tend to be cautious, somewhat withdrawn, and sometimes feel somewhat inferior to others around them.

Communication is one of the pathways to new experiences. Thus, adventurous individuals are less likely to have high levels of communication apprehension. They show more interest in communication and are likely to seek communication opportunities. Individuals low in adventurousness are more likely to be communication apprehensive and to withdraw from prospective communication experiences.

Neuroticism

Have you ever met a person who is changeable, who is friendly and pleasant one day but out-of-sorts the next, who is easily upset and annoyed in work or social settings? This person is likely a highly neurotic individual. When we use the term neurotic within this context, we are specifically referring to someone with a tendency toward mania (being really happy) and depression (being really sad). A person who is highly neurotic tends to rapidly fluctuate between mania and depression, while someone who is a low neurotic tends to be stable, calm, and well balanced most of the time.

Most low neurotic people enjoy communicating and show a much greater desire to communicate, greater flexibility in their communication, and greater adaptability to the moods of others with whom they are communicating. The less neurotic a person is, the less likely it is that he will be a high communication apprehensive. Highly neurotic people have difficulty just handling themselves without the increased pressure of relating to others. Thus, communication can become problematic for the highly neurotic individual. Such people are more likely to become high communication apprehensives.

Introversion/Extraversion

The person with an introverted personality tends to be shy and withdrawn and prefers to spend too much time alone. Generally, introverts find other people to have a limited appeal and are happier without them. At the other end of the personality continuum, extroverts are bold, aggressive, and talkative. They are much happier when they are with other people. Although introverts tend to have higher levels of communication apprehension, and extroverts tend to have lower levels of communication apprehension, this relationship is far from perfect. Some introverts have little or no apprehension about communicating; they simply prefer not to communicate because they simply do not care much for other people. They withdraw from communication, but they do so from preference rather than from fear. Similarly, some extroverts have fairly high levels of communication apprehension, but they are so people-oriented that they force themselves to communicate in spite of these fears. Consequently, we may sometimes mistake the introvert for the high communication apprehensive or the extrovert for the low communication apprehensive. Their communication behaviors are similar. The relationship between introversion and high communication apprehension is positive and moderately strong.

Self-Esteem

Self-esteem refers to the way a person evaluates herself in terms of overall self-worth. People with low self-esteem tend to feel they are not worthwhile; that they are more likely to fail than to succeed, and that they are less competent than other people around them. In contrast, people with high self-esteem see themselves as valuable members of society and as winners who are competent and likely to be successful.

People with low self-esteem tend to have higher levels of communication apprehension; people with high self-esteem tend to have lower levels of communication apprehension. Those in the latter group expect to succeed in their communication experiences, just as they expect to succeed in other ways. (Complete Appendix J to get your Self-Perceived Communication Competence score.) People with high self-esteem tend to be leaders in most communication environments, while those with low self-esteem tend to be followers.

A person with an adventurous personality tend to be more sociable and outgoing and have a lot of variability in their emotional responses.

Innovativeness

Innovativeness is the personality characteristic that refers to a person's willingness to change or accept change in the society around them. There is a strong negative relationship between an individual's innovativeness and level of communication apprehension. High levels of innovativeness tend to be associated with low levels of communication apprehension. People who are willing to introduce a change must be willing to communicate about that change. They also must be willing to accept challenges about the usefulness of the change. This makes it difficult for a high communication apprehensive to be innovative. As a consequence, high communication apprehensives might become resistant to change because change tends to require increased communication within their environment.

Tolerance for Disagreement

Tolerance for disagreement is an individual's tolerance for other people taking positions different from one's own. Some people are able to tolerate a high level of disagreement before they feel they are in conflict with another person, while others have a low level of such tolerance. For example, competitive debaters tend to have a high level of tolerance for disagreement because of their communication environment; debaters are constantly in disagreement with one another, hence in order to succeed, they must be able to handle this disagreement without taking it personally.

Tolerance for disagreement is negatively associated with communication apprehension. People with high levels of communication apprehension tend to have low levels of tolerance for disagreement. Because communication demands increase when disagreement is present, and they don't view communication as rewarding, even a small amount of disagreement can cause high communication apprehensives to perceive that they are in conflict with another person. At this point, high communication apprehensives have to choose between more communication or submission to the other person. Typically, they choose to submit. High communication apprehensives, then, tend to have a low tolerance for disagreement and usually try their best to avoid situations in which disagreement is likely to occur.

Assertiveness

Assertiveness refers to the way people assert or defend themselves and their rights as individuals. People with low assertiveness don't stand up for themselves and often get taken advantage of by others. People with high levels of assertiveness tend to get ahead and don't let others take advantage of them. This does not mean they are aggressive or rude; they simply stand their own ground. As you might have guessed, people with high assertiveness tend to have low levels of communication apprehension, and people with low assertiveness tend to have high levels.

Conclusions

From the relationships between communication apprehension and other personality characteristics discussed in this section, we are able to draw generalized profiles of the high and low communication apprehensive. The person who is highly communication apprehensive (scared to talk, quiet) tends to:

1. Suffer from general anxiety;
2. Have a low tolerance for ambiguity;
3. Lack of self-control;
4. Be unadventurous;
5. Lack emotional maturity;
6. Be introverted;
7. Have low self-esteem;
8. Be noninnovative;
9. Have a low tolerance for disagreement; and
10. Be unassertive.

On the other hand, the person who has a low level of communication apprehension (likes to talk, is usually outgoing) tends to:

1. Have low general anxiety;
2. Tolerate ambiguous situations;
3. Have a high degree of self-control;
4. Be adventurous;
5. Be emotionally mature;
6. Be extroverted;
7. Have high self-esteem;
8. Be innovative;
9. Be able to tolerate relatively high levels of disagreement; and
10. Be assertive.

Although these profiles, based on extensive research, are accurate in general, they do not necessarily apply to any single individual with either high or low communication apprehension. As we noted at the outset of this section, no two individuals have exactly the same personalities. The profiles we have outlined are useful to understanding the general ways both high and low communication apprehensives relate to other people and to their environment. This picture becomes much clearer upon examination of specific behavioral differences between high and low communication apprehensives, which we discuss in the following section.

Compulsive Communicators

Based on the preceding information, it would be easy to conclude that the talkative person is always a happy, well-adjusted model to emulate, and the quiet person is a poor, unfortunate soul who is to be pitied. This conclusion, drawn by many, is challenged by both quiet and talkative people. Many quiet people, when offered help to overcome their problems, respond with a firm "No, thank you!" They like themselves just the way they are. They have adjusted their lifestyles to accommodate their quietness and have no interest in changing. Some talkative persons, on the other hand, indicate that their supposedly ideal life is not all ideal. They complain that their propensity to approach all situations with an open mouth often gets them into trouble. Some find themselves in such high-powered, demanding positions that they are soon prime candidates for ulcers, migraine headaches, and heart attacks.

For example, compulsive communicators, or "talkaholics," are a special case of talkative people (McCroskey & Richmond, 1993). These people are not only highly talkative, but also are driven to talk. Talkaholics talk when they should talk, they talk when it makes no difference whether they do or not, and, most importantly, they talk when they should be quiet. Some are unable to determine when they should talk and when they should be quiet until it is too late. Others know they should keep quiet, but are simply unable to do so. Their overly talkative behavior is compulsive and beyond their control.

Talkaholics represent only a small proportion of the population. Our research suggests probably only one person in 20 (5% of the general population) is a talkaholic. Another 5% or 10% of the population may be borderline talkaholics. These are people who can control their talking behavior much of the time, but under certain circumstances or with certain people, they may lose control. Before we continue, turn to Appendix K. Complete the Talkaholic Scale (TAS) and score your responses. You probably had little difficulty completing the TAS, particularly if you are a talkaholic.

For the most part, talkaholics or compulsive-communicators are addicted or driven to talk. It is a compulsion, and they often cannot help themselves. They are often well aware that they have a problem with talking when they should not. Although they probably know that others view them as excessive talkers, they are not bothered by the perception.

They most likely were told that they talk too much on many occasions. In addition, they often recognize that they talked when they should have kept quiet or said something that they should not have said. Although recognition of their problem is one step toward controlling it, it is far from a solution.

As you read the above, you probably have in mind someone you know. Most people have no trouble identifying at least one acquaintance who they believe is a talkaholic. You should take care, however, not to presume everybody who talks too much is a talkaholic. Usually when we believe someone talks too much, it is not his quantity of talk that causes our concern. Rather, it is the quality of what he says. If that person spent her or his time telling someone else about your many virtues, you would be less likely to think that person talked too much.

DISCUSSION QUESTIONS

1. Through the years, a definition of communication apprehension has evolved. What is the most recent definition of communication apprehension? Who developed this definition?
2. How are writing apprehension and singing apprehension related to communication apprehension?
3. McCroskey posits four major types of communication apprehension. What are they? Give an example of each one.
4. How are pathological communication behaviors related to communication apprehension?
5. Communication apprehension is very much a part of a person's overall personality. How is apprehension related to the following: general anxiety, tolerance for ambiguity, self-control, adventurousness, emotional maturity, introversion, self-esteem, innovativeness, tolerance for disagreement, and assertiveness?
6. What are some behaviors of the typical talkative person versus the quiet person in the classroom setting?
7. How do quiet versus talkative persons select housing?
8. What occupational choices are available for those persons with a high WTC versus persons with a low WTC?
9. What are some causes of traitlike communication apprehension? What are the situational causes of communication anxiety?

ACTIVITIES

1. Complete the PRCA-24, the WAS, and the SAT and compare your scores on each measure.

2. Think of a speaking situation that causes you extreme anxiety, write a paragraph about the experience, and attempt to give suggestions for how to approach the situation the next time it arises.

3. Take the following four types of communication apprehension (trait-like, context-based, audience-based, and situational) and (1) give an example of where you felt anxious during each type or (2) describe how someone you know felt anxious when experiencing each type of CA.

4. The following are major causes of situational anxiety: novelty, formality, subordinate status, conspicuousness, unfamiliarity, dissimilarity, and degree of attention. Give an example when you have either experienced anxiety in each of the above or observed someone else experiencing anxiety in each of the above.

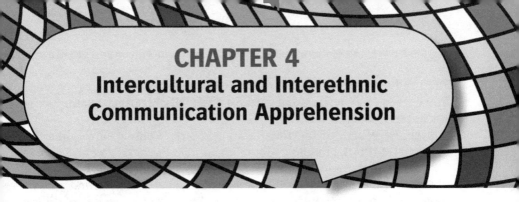

CHAPTER 4
Intercultural and Interethnic Communication Apprehension

Earlier in this book we discussed the importance that biology has on communication apprehension, but we should also stress that one's culture appears to have a clear impact on one's level of communication apprehension, shyness, and willingness to communicate. In this chapter, we explore the role that culture may or may not play in an individual's communication apprehension. First, we explore some of the theoretical problems associated with examining communication apprehension in various cultures. Second, we look at how communication apprehension affects our communication with others from differing cultures.

The Influence of Culture on Communication Apprehension

Research examining cross-cultural differences in communication apprehension dates back to the mid-1970s. By cross-cultural, we specifically refer to a comparison of two or more cultures. For example, do Japanese and Americans differ in their levels of communication apprehension? Or do Hawaiian Americans and mainland Americans differ in their levels of communication apprehension? In both cases, we compare fairly distinct cultures to one another to see if the individuals who live in those cultures differ in their levels of communication apprehension. We'll answer these questions later in this chapter. However, before we can discuss the research comparing differing cultures, we should discuss whether or not culture really matters.

Does Culture Matter?

Probably the researcher most synonymous with examining intercultural communication apprehension is Donald W. Klopf, who initiated the earliest cross-cultural studies of the subject in the mid-1970s. Klopf spent a great deal of his life as a researcher teaching at the University of Hawaii at Manoa. During his time at the university, he published over 20 articles specifically examining cross-cultural communication, and many of these articles focus on how different cultures differ with regards to communication apprehension.

Over the course of the three editions of the volume now edited by Daly et al. (2009), *Avoiding Communication: Shyness, Reticence, and Communication Apprehension*, Klopf discussed the changing nature of cross-cultural communication apprehension research. In the first edition published in 1984, the focus was more on the differences or lack of differences Klopf had found between different cultures. By the second edition published in 1997, Klopf still discussed the various differences that had been seen among different cultures around the globe related to communication apprehension, but his and others' research was more tempered and cautionary. Specifically, Klopf wondered if the lack of interest in cross-cultural communication apprehension research stemmed "from the fact that not every culture prizes oral skills as does the U.S. culture. Israel does and so do the British. Australia, Korea, and the Philippines, among others, reward oral behavior. Nevertheless, for every culture placing a premium on verbalizing aloud, there are others not so included. In many Asian and African cultures, speech is less valued" (p. 269). He even noted that within the United States, many co-cultures (e.g., Native Americans from the Apache nation, Quakers, etc.) avoid speech in certain contexts. In essence, Klopf warned that many communication researchers viewed human communication from a primarily Western rhetorical tradition, which discounts the communication experiences of people in other cultures.

By the time the third edition of Daly et al.'s (2009) synthesis of the research on communication apprehension was published, Klopf became even more hesitant about the importance of cross-cultural communication apprehension research. This time his focus examined what he referred to as "hegemonic Eurocentrism," or the notion that communication apprehension research was predominantly conducted from a Western perspective that may not necessarily align itself with other cultural perspectives. Klopf cites Kim (2002), who wrote, "without information about a culture's general predisposition toward verbal communication, research on CA in a given culture may not be very useful" (p. 34). In essence, differing global cultures place greater or less emphasis on verbal communication in life. As such, saying that communication apprehension is a negative construct in all cultures and comparing American's levels of communication apprehension against other cultures may not fundamentally make sense. According to cultural researchers Geert Hofstede and Gert Jan Hofstede, Eurocentric cultures are generally more individualistic, which represents a "society in which the ties between individuals are loose: everyone is expected to look after himself or herself and his or her immediate family only" (Hofstede & Hofstede, 2005, p. 401).

From a Eurocentric perspective, the notion of "rhetoric" dates back to the ancient Greeks where the focus was purely on persuasion and speech making. Today, we use a broader definition of rhetoric that "involves the use of symbols to achieve responses from humans, a study that covers verbal and nonverbal strategies used to influence people" (Klopf, 2009, p. 243). However, even our more modern conceptualization of rhetoric is still deeply rooted in Western ideas of logical, analytical, and rational thinking. As Klopf (2009) notes, "In the Eurocentric style, the primary function of speaking is to express ideas and thoughts as clearly, logically, and persuasively as possible in an individualistic fashion. Speakers are expected to be direct, explicit, and exact. Silence should be avoided, and speakers are expected to say what they mean and mean what they say . . . Apprehensive speakers find no solace in that atmosphere" (p. 243).

An Asiancentric perspective, on the other hand, stems out of what Hofstede and Hofstede (2005) call collectivism, which "stands for a society in which people from birth onward are integrated into strong, cohesive in-groups, which throughout people's lifetime continue to protect them in exchange for unquestioning loyalty" (p. 399). In collectivism, the "group's fate is more important than the individual's fate, and the individual is subservient to the group" (Klopf, 2009, p. 244). As such, it should not be surprising that communication in collectivistic cultures is distinctly different from communication in individualistic cultures. Based on Klopf's analysis of Asiancentric communication we can analyze six general beliefs about communication that differ from Eurocentric beliefs.

First, Asiancentric cultures believe that the words one uses can alter meaning from one communication encounter to the next. There is more emphasis on the subtlety and word meanings "are thought to be particular, implying that total understanding with another person requires mental unification with that person. Oneness or perfect harmony is suggested by that belief, and that tenant represents all major Eastern religions" (Klopf, 2009, p. 244).

Second, Asiancentric cultures do not believe that an embellishment of language is necessary for communication. Although Eurocentric communication styles focus on the use of language and where many conflate quantity of communication with quality of communication. In Asiancentric cultures, the use of silence is often as important as the use of words. In Eurocentric communication, silence is often referred to as "dead air" or the proverbial "lull in the conversation" and is generally frowned upon.

Third, Klopf (2009) notes that Asiancentric cultures have a tendency to accentuate status during one's interactions with others. Where Eurocentric cultures tend to be more focused on the young, Asiancentric cultures honor their elders and communication with one's elders or people higher in the social hierarchy than one's self should be more formal.

Fourth, there is often a belief in Asiancentric cultures that an individual's relationships with other people, not their use of words, that will be most important when attempting to accomplish one's communication goals. As Klopf (2009) noted, "Asians are usually more concerned with an interaction's emotional quality than with the meaning of particular words or sentences. A successful speech act does not rely on well-developed informational content and reasoning with evidence; it relies on maintaining the relationship through the use of culturally mandated styles or by establishing the speaker's character by indicating good deeds" (p. 245). Ultimately, "character precedes arguments, style precedes contents, and relationships precede actions" (Klopf, 2009, p. 245).

Fifth, Asiancentric cultures tend to suppress conflict and avoid negative messages, especially with one's friends and family. In essence, being courteous to people in your friendship circle or family is considerably more important than being truthful. If truth could lead to unpleasantness or hurt another person's feelings, Asiancentric individuals will avoid those topics and ultimately seem more reserved in order to avoid hurting the other person's social face. Tjosvold, Hui, and Sun (2000) define social face as "Social face then can be defined as the image of strength persons want to project in conflict. Showing respect to people confirms face in that it communicates an acceptance of this positive image whereas disrespect affronts face" (p. 5). Therefore, individuals in Asiancentric cultures are more concerned with maintaining someone's positive social face than with being bluntly honest, which is often seen as an attribute of Eurocentric cultures.

Last, Klopf notes that Asiancentric communication is "intuitive, empathetic, silent, reserved, and subtle" (2009, p. 245). In essence, where Eurocentric cultures are focused more on what comes out of one's mouth, Asiancentric cultures are more concerned with the thought process that occurs before communication is actually attempted.

Admittedly, Klopf warns that these six distinctions of Asiancentric communication are clearly based on broad strokes and generalizations about Asiancentric cultures as a whole, so clearly differences will occur across different geographic regions. Furthermore, this has an impact on our understanding of communication apprehension in so far as our understanding as Eurocentric scholars is going to cloud our perception of communication. Eurocentric scholars are more likely to value talk and the importance of talk within society because their culture values talk more. However, when researchers start analyzing communication patterns (especially those of shy people) across cultures, researchers are often only seeing Western perceptions of the importance of talk and not necessarily the perceptions of the importance of talk in other cultures. Ultimately, this leads Klopf to suggest that emphasis on cultural differences in communication apprehension research should be done cautiously.

Examining Cultural Differences

Now that we've examined some of Klopf's (2009) hesitations to conducting cross-cultural communication apprehension research, we can examine what some of that research has looked like. Over the years, the Personal Report of Communication Apprehension (PRCA, Appendix F) has been handed out in a wide range of differing cultures. Many of these cultures were non-native English speaking cultures or non-English speaking cultures completely. When conducting cross-cultural communication research using a measure like the PRCA, one must take a number of steps to translate the measure into a new language. There are many different techniques researchers can use to translate measures (see Wrench, Thomas-Maddox, Richmond, and McCroskey (2019)), but the most common way is to take the original English version of the scale and give it to a bilingual individual. This individual can take the PRCA and then translate the measure into the secondary language. Ideally, you'll then have a second bilingual individual who then takes the newly translated version of the measure and translates it back into English. If the original version of the English measure reads the same as the retranslated version of the measure, then you probably have a well-translated measure. If, however, the two are vastly different, then a translation problem has occurred. Even if you follow these steps, one problem that often plagues translations involves cultural idioms. Cultural idioms are those little sayings that have special meaning within a culture that when translated take on a separate meaning because there is no cultural reference for the translation. For example, if we translated the phrase "out in left field" to Russian, you'll get "Выход в левом поле." However, the phrase "out in left field" refers to baseball and without the understanding of this idea, research participants in other cultures may not be able to understand the meaning of the phrase. Furthermore, sometimes a literal translation actually alters the meaning. For example, when one directly translates "Выход в левом поле" back into English, the direct translation becomes "Exit in left field." Clearly, the literal translation and the cultural understanding of the words get lost. So, in addition to working on the basic translation of words, you also need to ensure that the general idea being communicated is also being translated at the same time.

Starting back in the mid-1970s and continuing to the present day, scholars around the world have conducted research to examine differences among various groups with regards to communication apprehension and willingness to communicate. We also avoided using studies that were based completely on examining CA levels and international students in Table 4.1 because those research participants are probably not overly representative of those cultures. Although not all studies have examined both of these variables, Table 4.1 provides means for the different groups.

Cultural Group	CA	WTC
Possible Score Ranges	**24–120**	**0–100**
Australia	60.37	56.06
Argentina	74.47	
China	79.8	
Finland	65.08	54.06
France	84.66	73.54
Germany	73.14	
Guam	60.78	
Ireland	63.02	
Iranian Kurdistan	57.36	
Japan	65.90	
Malaysia	71.03	
Micronesia	60.78	47.03
New Zealand	65.07	60.08
Philippines	58.09	
Puerto Rico	59.00	72.06
Russian	65.08	48.04
Spain	64.26	
Singapore (Ethnic Chinese)	53.17	60.57
Singapore (Malay Immigrants)	36.13	54.52
South Korea	52.78	
Sweden	62.40	58.01
Switzerland	65.85	
Thailand	71.05	
Taiwan	70.92	63.38
United Kingdom	64.16	
United States	65.06*	63.01
University of Hawaii Students at Manoa	62.35	
African Americans	59.09	
Hispanic/Latino	67.06	

* Based on normative data from McCroskey, Fayer, and Richmond (1985)

Table 4.1 *Means of Cultural Groups on CA & WTC*

The means in Table 4.1 were taken from a variety of different studies, so they cannot be used for comparison purposes alone. Instead, we need to examine the individual studies to see which groups can be directly compared with one another. Obviously, the United States has been compared to more of these cultures than any other, so starting our analysis with the United States makes sense.

United States of America. A variety of different studies have compared CA scores between the United States and other cultures. Specifically, the following countries have been shown to have greater communication apprehension levels when compared with the United States: China, Micronesia, Japan, New Zealand, Russia, and Taiwan. The following cultures had scores lower than the United States on CA: Australia, Guam, South Korea, and Puerto Rico. Last, the following countries scores on CA were similar those of the United States: Argentina, Finland, and Sweden.

Furthermore, we have data comparing the United States to those of other cultures on WTC. No countries had greater WTC scores than the United States. The following cultures had scores lower than those of the United States on WTC: China, Finland, Micronesia, Japan, New Zealand, Russia, Sweden, and Taiwan.

We should note that research conducted in the United States comparing University of Hawaii Students and mainland college students did find that Hawaiian students reported significantly higher levels of CA when compared with their mainland counterparts. Furthermore, University of Hawaiian students were less willing to communicate than their mainland counterparts.

Australia. A great deal of cross-cultural comparison data has come from examining CA between Australia and various countries. Specifically, the following countries have been shown to have greater communication apprehension levels when compared with Australia: Japan, Sweden, and the United States. The following cultures had scores lower than Australia on CA: Korea and the Philippines. Last, the following countries scores on CA were similar to Australia: China, Finland, Micronesia, and Russia.

China. A number of studies have compared communication apprehension levels between individuals living in mainland China and other cultures. Specifically, only Japan has greater communication apprehension levels when compared with those of China. The following cultures had scores lower than China on CA: Koreans. Last, the following countries scores on CA were similar to those of China: Australia, Guam, Micronesia, Korea, Philippines, and the United States.

Japan. The second most commonly studied culture with regards to CA has been Japan. Specifically, no countries have been shown to have greater communication apprehension levels when compared to Japan. The following cultures had scores lower than those of Japan on CA: Australia, China, Guam, Korea, Micronesia, Philippines, Puerto Rico, and the United States.

Korea. Although we use the general term "Korea" within this section, we are specifically relating to data collected from South Korea. Although the South and North Korean people may be similar, we do not want to overgeneralize our findings to both countries here. All of the countries studied in conjunction with Korea have been shown to have greater levels of CA: Australia, China, Hawaii, Japan, Micronesia, Philippines, and the United States.

Micronesia. A considerable number of studies have examined communication apprehension in Micronesia. Specifically, the following countries have been shown to have greater communication apprehension levels when compared with Micronesia's: Japan and the United States. The following cultures had scores lower than Micronesia's on CA: Korea, Philippines, and Puerto Rico. Last, the following countries scores on CA were similar to Micronesia's: Australia, China, Finland, Hawaii, and Russia.

Philippines. The Philippines have been studied in conjunction with a number of different cultures with regards to communication. Although research has found that people in the Philippines have higher levels of CA when compared those of Koreans, they are generally lower than other cultures including Americans, Australians, Chinese, Micronesians, and Japanese.

Single Comparison Studies. In addition to the above series of research that analyzed different cultures' levels of CA against one another, a whole series of research has examined only two groups. For example, in a study comparing United Kingdom accounting students to those in Spain, the researchers found that the UK students had higher levels of CA when compared with their Spanish counterparts (Arquero, Hassall, Joyce, & Donoso, 2007). In another study conducted by Bolls and Tan (1996), the researchers examined the impact that communication apprehension had in the classroom comparing Native American and Caucasian students. The researchers found that Native American elementary school students reported higher fear of classroom communication than their Caucasian counterparts.

In 2015 Croucher, Sommier, Rahmani, and Appenrodt, examined CA differences between England, Finland, and Germany. Overall, the study found that those living in England reported lower levels of CA when compared to those living in Finland or Germany. The study did not find any specific differences between those living in Finland and Germany, however.

Overall, this line of research has shown some interesting differences in levels of communication apprehension across various cultures. However, the ultimate ramification of these results should be tempered as suggested by Klopf (2009).

Cultural Influences on Communication Apprehension

Although the first part of this chapter focused on how different cultures scored on their levels of CA, the rest of this chapter will focus on an individual's level of CA with regards to interacting with people from other cultures. For our purposes, we define culture as "a group of people who through a process of learning are able to share perceptions of the world that influences their beliefs, values, norms, and rules, which eventually affect behavior" (Wrench et al., 2008, p. 421). As such, the word "culture" is a broad term that encompasses (1) how we learn about our world, (2) how we think about the world, and (3) how we communicate and behave within the world. When people think about "culture," they often immediately think of nationalistic cultures or how the United States is different from New Zealand, Tawain, Russia, etc. . . . However, we should also be aware of various co-cultures that also exist. Co-cultures are "cultural groups not necessarily below or suppressed by the larger culture, but existing inside of a larger culture" (Wrench et al., 2008, p. 421). When we talk about co-cultures within the United States, one example could be religious co-cultures (Protestants, Catholics, Mormons, Jews, Muslims, Buddhists, etc.). Within the United States, we have numerous types of co-cultures that exist relating to geographical location within our country, sexual orientation, age, income-level, ethnic identification (e.g., Italian American, Irish American, Turkish American, Latino/Hispanic, etc.), education,

Intercultural communication in the United States (U.S.) is virtually unavoidable.

Syda Productions/Shutterstock.com

etc. . . . . In each of these different cultural contexts, you will experience differences in how members learned about our world, think about the world, and communicate and behave within the world.

Berger and Calabrese (1975) created a theory for understanding communication during initial interactions called uncertainty reduction theory (URT). URT theorizes that when two people first meet there will be a high degree of uncertainty between those two individuals. Because of this uncertainty, people will communicate with one another in an attempt to reduce this uncertainty in an effort to make the other person seem more predictable. We make other people more predictable through both information seeking (we ask questions about the other person in an effort to learn cognitive facts and see how they communicate and behave), and we use nonverbal affiliative expressiveness (nonverbal actions [e.g., eye contact, facial expressions, gesturing, smiling, and touching] people use to demonstrate their connection and closeness to another person). Because people from different cultures bring along an even greater degree of uncertainty, combined with the fact that information seeking and knowing appropriate affiliative expressive behavior may be altered by language or cultural differences, these interactions are often rife with novelty, unfamiliarity, dissimilarity, and uncertainty.

Gudykunst and Kim (2002) note that when someone approaches another person from a differing culture they tend to view each other as "strangers." As such, when interacting with someone from another culture, the more dissimilar that culture is from your own the greater the degree of "strangeness" and unfamiliar that interaction will encounter. Thus, there will be more unfamiliarity and uncertainty with people from other cultures and co-cultures than with people from our own cultures and co-cultures. As such, for some people this heightened level of dissimilarity and uncertainty can actually lead some individuals to experience anxiety while communicating with someone from a differing culture or co-culture.

Research examining the impact of CA and WTC on intercultural interactions has found that both impact how people view themselves interculturally. Research by Hsu (2010) examined a group of Chinese Americans and found that an individual's level of communication apprehension made them less likely to adopt an American identity, and when they did interact with others they self-disclosed information at a much lower level than their more talkative counterparts. Of course, one of the ways we reduce our uncertainty during intercultural encounters is through information seeking and exchange, so if someone is less willing to disclose information about himself, it's only going to perpetuate the feeling of strangeness.

Another interesting sidebar for CA research involving intercultural issues has been on the differences between first- and second-language CA. Imagine you're a first-generation Turkish American and your first language (the one you grew up speaking) is Turkish. After immigrating to the United States you learn English, and English quickly becomes your second language. Some researchers have sought to determine if there is a difference between an individual's levels of CA in his first and second languages and whether these differences have an impact on communication in distinct patterns. In a study by Richmond, McCroskey, McCroskey, and Fayer (2008), the researchers examined a group of Puerto Rican students who all spoke Spanish as a first language and English as a second language. The goal of this study was to examine whether people would respond different to measures of CA, WTC, shyness, talkaholism, and sociocommunicative orientation when thinking about their first or their second language. For this study, the results were virtually identical for first and second languages. However, previous research noted that Puerto Ricans tend to have low levels of CA in their first languages and high levels of CA in their second languages.

Jung and McCroskey (2004) also examined 120 international students who did not speak English as a first language. They found that an individual's level of CA in their first language was positive related to their level of CA in their second language, so quiet people are going to be quiet people no matter what language they are speaking. Interestingly enough, an individual's level of CA in English did reduce with the number of years a person had been speaking English. In essence, the more one was exposed to speaking English, the more communicatively competent the person became, which corresponded in a reduction of CA while speaking English.

The rest of this section is going to explore three different aspects related to CA in intercultural communication: intercultural CA, interethnic CA, and CA in other cultural contexts.

Intercultural Communication Apprehension

As noted by Neuliep and McCroskey (1997), "intercultural communication in the United States (U.S.) is virtually unavoidable... The U.S. is in the midst of the largest and most extensive wave of cultural mixing in history" (p. 147). Neuliep and McCroskey go on to note that effective intercultural CA is important in the United States today more so than at any other time in history, "the political and economic effectiveness of the U.S. depends on the individual and collective abilities to communicate competently with people from different cultures" (p. 147). As such, learning how to communicate with people from other cultures is necessary for anyone in modern business or politics and just about any occupation. However, knowing the negative effects that CA can have in other contexts, Neuliep and McCroskey believed that intercultural CA could have equally damaging effects on an individual's ability to communicate with people from differing cultures and co-cultures.

The Personal Report of Intercultural Communication Apprehension (PRICA, Appendix L) was developed to measure an individual's level of fear or anxiety associated with either real or anticipated communication with another person or persons from a differing culture or co-culture. Intercultural communication apprehension (ICA) is a relatively new endeavor for communication researchers only dating back to the mid-1990s, so there isn't nearly as much research on the subject as there is general communication apprehension. However, what research we have conducted clearly depicts a problematic picture.

Probably the single most important result that has been consistently found related to ICA has been its positive relationship with ethnocentrism. Ethnocentrism is the idea that one's culture is centrally important, so all other cultures should be judged and evaluated based on one's culture. The highly ethnocentric individual will judge all other cultures or co-cultures in comparison with her or his own particular culture or co-culture, especially with concern to behavior, communicative practices, customs, language, religion, and rituals. When one looks at the bulk of the conflicts in the world today, most of them stem out of ethnocentrism. Because of the strong relationship between one's level of ICA and ethnocentrism, we can be certain that a good chunk of one's apprehension stems from a place of cultural judgment, which in turn will actually have an impact on an individual's intercultural communication behavior.

Neuliep and Ryan (1998) examined the impact that ICA has on intercultural behaviors by pairing U.S. students with international communication partners. After initial interactions, they found that individuals (on both the United States and international side of the conversation) who had high ICA levels had more uncertainty about future interactions with their cross-cultural communication partner and were less certain of their own feelings about their cross-cultural communication partner. Furthermore, ICA was found to negatively relate to both factors of sociocommunicative orientation (assertiveness and responsiveness). For communication purposes, both assertiveness and responsiveness have been shown to help with the information exchange part of Berger and Calabrese's theory of uncertainty reduction in initial interactions. In a study conducted by Lin and Rancer (2003), they found that individuals who had high levels of ICA were less willing to communicate interculturally and less desire to interact with people in an intercultural dialogue program.

Wrench, Corrigan, McCroskey, and Punyanunt-Carter (2006) studied ICA in terms of how it has an impact on religious communication. The researchers found that individuals with high levels of ICA were less tolerant of religious disagreement. The higher my ICA score the more I believe that others should adapt and adhere to my religious views, which clearly stems out of ethnocentrism. Furthermore, the researchers found that individuals with high levels of ICA were also less tolerant of bisexual, gay, and lesbian (BGL) individuals as well, which is another clear indication of the impact that ethnocentrism has on an individual's level of ICA.

Interestingly, results comparing females with males on ICA, ethnocentrism, and anti-BGL attitudes consistently show men having higher levels of all three. One theory for why men have higher ICA, ethnocentrism, and anti-BGL attitudes stems out of critical theory. Critical theory, at its basic level, examines power imbalances within our world. Historically, in Western society, men have maintained leadership in economics, politics, and religion. Any person who is viewed as a "stranger" is viewed as a threat to power. As such, from this theoretical perspective men have more to lose as equality occurs and our society becomes more diverse, and so men are more judgmental of anyone they view as different, which is clearly based in ethnocentrism. Now, we are not saying that *all* men have high levels of ICA, ethnocentrism, and anti-BGL attitudes, but when we compare men with women within the United States, this pattern consistently emerges.

The flipside to ICA is an individual's intercultural willingness to communicate (IWTC). Lin and Rancer (2003) found that individuals with a high IWTC were more likely to participate in intercultural dialogue programs. Furthermore, individuals with high ITWC had lower levels of ethnocentrism.

Overall, these results definitely show that having high levels of ICA are a detriment to one's intercultural encounters. Although ICA may be strongly related to ethnocentrism as a general concept, there is still a relationship between ICA and CA levels. Future research should really attempt to parcel out what is truly just an individual's level of CA and what is ICA.

Interethnic Communication Apprehension

"Ethnicity" is one of those terms misused by many within our society and often used synonymously with the word "race." For our purposes, we refer to ethnicity as representing a classifying scheme that labels a group with similar geographical or cultural traditions (e.g., African Americans, Korean Americans, Mexican Americans, Italian Americans, Kenyan Americans, etc.). These co-cultural groups differ in how members learn about our world, think about the world, and communicate and behave within the world. Although they are still affected by the larger culture of the United States, these differing ethnic groups hold on to and are affected by their own ethnic co-cultures.

The Personal Report of Interethnic Communication Apprehension (PRECA, Appendix M) was developed to measure an individual's level of fear or anxiety associated with either real or anticipated communication with another person or persons from a differing ethnicity. Interethnic communication apprehension IECA is also based out of one's level of ethnocentrism and positively related to one's level of CA. Furthermore, men once again have been shown to have higher levels of IECA when compared with their female counterparts.

Toale and McCroskey (2001) examined the effects that IECA has on the use of relational maintenance strategies during interethnic interactions. Overall, individuals with high IECA scores were less likely to use relational maintenance strategies with interethnic communication partners. In essence, people with high levels of IECA simply did not put as much effort into building or attempting to start a relationship with an interethnic communication partner as did people with lower levels of interethnic communication apprehension. In another study by Bippus and Dorjee (2002) found that individuals with high levels of IECA before engaging in a dialogue with someone from a different ethnicity were less satisfied with their communication after the fact. Clearly, one's level of IECA has a negative effect on his ability to have successful and fulfilling interethnic communication relationships.

Communication Apprehension in Other Cultural Contexts

So far in this chapter we've focused on intercultural and interethnic communication apprehension. In recent years a couple of new lines of research have been initiated to examine the impact that communication has in other cultural contexts.

First, in 2008 Punyanunt-Carter, Wrench, Corrigan, and McCroskey developed the Religious Communication Apprehension Measure (Appendix N) to examine the "anxiety or fear associated with either real or anticipated interaction about religion with people of other religions" (p. 2). They also examined an individual's willingness to communicate about religion with other people who may have a different religion. Overall, the researchers found that people with higher levels of religious communication apprehension (RCA) had lower levels of willingness to communicate about religion (RWTC), which is not surprising. Furthermore, people with high levels of RCA were more anxious about receiving information about someone else's religion than people with low levels of RCA. Of course, people with high levels of RWTC had lower levels of anxiety listening to someone else's religious information. Last, people with high levels of RCA had lower levels of tolerance for those who presented religious ideas that differed from their own. Of course, people with high RWTC were more tolerant of religious ideas that differed from their own.

In a follow-up study by Punyanunt-Carter, Corrigan, Wrench, and McCroskey (2010), the researchers examined RCA and RWTC in terms of political affiliations and biological sex. In this study, Republicans and Democrats had similar levels of RCA and RWTC. Furthermore, females and males had similar levels of RCA or RWTC, which shows that in the case of RCA and RWTC, these concepts are functioning differently from other forms of CA in terms of biological sex. Of course, this is just one study, so other research would need to confirm this finding.

In a second follow up study, Arias, Punyanunt-Carter, and Wrench (2017) further examined the relationship between RCA and religious receiver apprehension (RRA). The authors found individuals who had a high tolerance for religious disagreements were shown to have lower levels of RRA and higher levels of RCA. Furthermore, individuals with high levels of RRA had more negative attitudes toward various forms of evangelism.

The final pair of studies we want to talk about here takes communication apprehension in a completely new and different "cultural" direction.

Co-cultural groups differ in how members learn about our world, think about the world, and communicate and behave within the world.

In Nass and Yen's (2010) book *The Man Who Lied to His Laptop*, the authors discuss how humans have an interesting tendency to think, relate, and communicate with computers as they would other humans. Although we are not going to discuss this in terms of computer-mediated communication or how people use technology to interact with other humans here, we will examine these thoughts more in Chapter 5. Instead, here we're talking about human-computer interaction, or how humans interact and communicate with technology. Specifically, we're going to discuss human-robot communication apprehension.

In a study by Nomura, Suzuki, Kanda, and Kato (2006), the researchers examined if an individual's level of communication apprehension could account for his level of anxiety about robots. In this study, the PRCA-24 was utilized as the measure of CA and was not shown to relate to generalized anxiety about robots. In a subsequent study by Kido, Kim, Sur, Hendrickson, and Doi (2008), these researchers reframed the idea of CA in relation to robots by specifically thinking about it in terms of intercultural communication. In this study, the authors reframed the interaction between humans and robots in terms of interethnic CA (I guess we'll call them Robot Americans). Using an ethnically diverse sample at the University of Hawaii, the researchers found that individuals with higher levels of interethnic CA also reported higher levels of anxiety when interacting with a robot. Furthermore, individuals with high Robot CA also reported more negative attitudes toward robots, which could once again be a further indication of the impact of ethnocentrism on interethnic CA. Last, individuals who had higher levels of CA also were more individualistic in their cultural outlooks and less collectivistic to refer back to Hofstede and Hofstede's (2005) work. Although it may be hard to think of robots in terms of culture, could our own cultures have an impact on how we view our interactions with robots culturally? These results definitely suggest this can happen.

Conclusion

This chapter has explored the world of intercultural communication and its relationship to communication apprehension. The chapter started by looking at the importance of culture within human communication and cultural differences in communication apprehension research. The chapter then examined the findings from a number of studies that have compared differing nationalistic cultures to one another with regards to CA. The chapter then moved on and looked at how communication apprehension can have an impact on our intercultural encounters with both other people and finally robots.

DISCUSSION QUESTIONS

1. Klopf (2009) discusses that one of the problems with cross-cultural CA research involves the Eurocentric versus Asiacentric focuses. Because of the cultural diversity within the United States, do you think Klopf's argument that the United States is Eurocentric is completely accurate?

2. Look at the list of countries where CA comparison cross-cultural research has been conducted (given in the section "Examining Cultural Differences"). Are you surprised by any of the findings? Why? Do these findings support Klopf's ideas on Eurocentrism versus Asiacentrism discussed at the beginning of the chapter?

3. Do you think there are certain co-cultures within your own culture that would cause you more apprehension than others? Why do you think these specific co-cultures provoke more anxiety?

4. How do you think intercultural CA affects information seeking and affiliative behaviors during initial interactions with an individual in an intercultural dialogue?

5. Although still a relatively under-researched concept, religious CA definitely appears to be functionally different than intercultural or interethnic CA. Why do you think some people are more apprehensive discussing religion than other parts of their lives?

6. Is human-robotic communication just another intercultural interaction? Why do you think the research on human-robotic communication is so similar to CA research examining human-to-human interethnic CA?

ACTIVITIES

1. Complete the PRICA, PRECA, and RCA scale and compare your scores on each measure.

2. Find a place on campus where international students tend to congregate. Try to start up a conversation with one of these students and then write a paragraph about your experience.

3. Contact your local international students' center and ask if they are looking for dialogue partners and volunteer if they need partners. Keep a journal of your experiences interacting with your dialogue partner. How does your level of intercultural communication apprehension change as you engage with an intercultural dialogue partner over time? Discuss with your intercultural dialogue partner her or his own communication apprehension when communicating with people from your culture.

4. Find someone from a religion that is distinctly different from your own (not just a different sect from within your own religion). Ask that individual about the importance of communication within her or his religion. Write a paragraph or two explaining your findings and how your own religious CA influences you during this interaction?

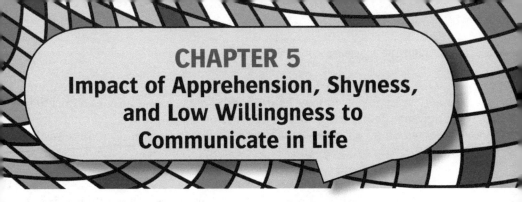

CHAPTER 5
Impact of Apprehension, Shyness, and Low Willingness to Communicate in Life

Behaviors of Quiet and Talkative People

We noted previously that the main impact of communication apprehension is anxiety about communicating with others and that one's willingness to communicate is the tendency to seek or avoid communication with others. Being a high CA, having a low willingness to communicate, or being perceived of as shy might have a major impact on an individual's lifestyle. People with low willingness to communicate (quiet persons) tend to avoid or withdraw from situations that will require communication. People with high willingness to communicate (talkative persons) tend to seek opportunities to communicate with other people. In this section, we review how these general tendencies influence behavior in specific situations and settings.

Classroom Setting

The classroom is a major communication environment. As such, it is not surprising that behaviors of quiet persons differ distinctly from the not-so-quiet individuals in the classroom.

To begin with, high and low communication apprehensives, when given free choice, make different decisions concerning what classes to take. Low communication apprehensives prefer classes with small enrollments where there is ample opportunity for students to interact with each other and with the instructor. High communication apprehensives, in contrast, tend to avoid such small classes in favor of larger, lecture-type classes in which the instructor talks to the students, and the students simply listen and take notes.

What the student is expected to contribute to the class in terms of communication also influences an individual's choice of classes. Classes that require oral reports or speeches are avoided by quiet persons but are attractive to talkative persons. Similarly, classes that base part of the final grade on "class participation" are attractive to communicative persons but understandably are disliked by uncommunicative persons.

Once a student is enrolled in a class, whether voluntarily or by require-ment, we might assume the student will simply accept the communication requirements and try to do his best. Such an assumption is incorrect. Quiet students often will drop a class with high communication requirements, even if it is a required course. For example, one study found that over 50% of the students with high communication apprehension dropped a required public-speaking course during the first three weeks of the course, just before the first speech was due to be presented. Other studies found that high communication apprehensives who remain in courses with high communication requirements are likely to be absent on days when they are scheduled for presentations. This finding is true not only at the college and high school levels but also at the elementary school level where "show and tell," "see and say," or "book report" assignments are required. Young children often claim they are unable to read so they can avoid having to read aloud to the class.

Talkative students are likely to engage in similar behaviors if there is little opportunity for communication in the course. Their attendance in lecture classes is likely to be low; they would rather get the neces-sary information by reading or talking to other students than by sitting through "all those lectures." Similarly, research has indicated that stu-dents with a high willingness to communicate do not like automated, individualized instruction situations in which they are given objectives, reading, or viewing assignments and tests with no opportunity for inter-action with a live teacher. They are likely to avoid or withdraw from the class or as an alternative, if they must have the class, complete it as quickly as possible.

Where a person chooses to sit in a classroom also reflects her or his level of quietness. Low communication apprehensives tend to sit in the front and center of the traditional classroom. High communication apprehen-sives tend to sit along the sides and in the rear of the room. Most inter-action in the typical classroom is focused on the center of the room in the first few rows. This is where the low apprehensive chooses to sit, and where the high communication apprehensive tries her or his best to avoid.

In addition, Ericson and Gardner (1992) have confirmed results of other researchers that over a standard 4-year period to complete a baccalaure-ate degree "there was a significant difference where the high communica-tion apprehensive student had a tendency not to complete her/his degree" (p. 131). At the institution they studied, Ericson and Gardner found that more than half the students they had classified as high communication apprehensives did not complete their degrees. They also found that for two consecutive years of incoming college freshmen "more high CA stu-dents dropped out than low CA students" (p. 132). Hence, the person with high communication apprehension (low willingness to communicate) is less likely to complete the standard four-year college program than the student with low communication apprehension.

Finally, type and amount of participation in the class are both affected by levels of quietness. Communicative students frequently volunteer to participate, even if they are not certain they know the correct answer.

Uncommunicative students will almost never volunteer to participate, even if they are certain they know the correct answer. In some instances, they even will knowingly give a wrong answer when called upon because they think that will decrease their chances of being called upon at a later date. Recent research with college students demonstrated that when high CA students were told to recall information given in a class lecture for another classmate, they lost approximately 20% of the information. Their recall dropped sharply in contrast to the classes in which other high CA students were not told they would have to communicate later. In other words, when the high CA college student thinks he or she will be asked to talk to a classmate and recall classroom content, the anxiety about communication interferes with her or his cognitive learning and later recall of what is taught. In short, willingness to communicate and apprehension have a direct impact on student preferences for classroom instruction and on student behaviors in the classroom. In most instances, the tendencies of high communication apprehensives push them toward behaviors that decrease their likelihood for success in the academic setting, but the tendencies of low communication apprehensives push them toward behaviors that increase their likelihood of success.

Small Group Settings

Although a small group discussion setting is less threatening to most people than is a public-speaking setting, and particularly so to a person with low willingness to communicate, this setting still places rather high communication demands on an individual. Consequently, it is not surprising that quiet people typically attempt to avoid small group communication or rather to sit quietly in a group if they must be present. Talkative persons, of course, tend to enjoy such experiences, to participate fully, or even to dominate the group. They frequently volunteer to serve on committees, even to chair them.

Although less talk on the part of a highly anxious person in a small group is predictable from our earlier discussions, some of the other behaviors in which high communication apprehensives have been found to engage are not as predictable. For example, not only do they talk less, they also say things that are less relevant to the ongoing discussion. It appears that this behavior has been learned as a means of getting people to stop asking the quiet person questions. Additionally, the number of times high communication apprehensives answer "I don't know" is disproportionately high compared to other group members.

Finally, both low and high apprehensives seem to have an innate ability to figure out where to sit in a small group setting in order to either facilitate or inhibit their communication. Research has indicated that high willing to communicate persons choose seats that facilitate interaction and lead to their taking on leadership function. On the other hand, low willing to communicate persons choose seats that inhibit communication and denote low status and power.

Dyadic/Interpersonal Settings

The behavior of quiet versus talkative persons in dyadic or interpersonal relationships (relationships between two people) differs sharply, as it does in other settings. In general, high willing to communicate people assume a dominant, leadership role, while low willing to communicate people assume a submissive, follower role.

The insecurity of the quiet person is reflected by the very low amount of self-disclosure in which they engage. They prefer not to talk about themselves. In addition, they seem overly concerned with being certain that the other dyadic member understands or agrees with them. They use a disproportionately large number of expressions, known as "rhetorical interrogatives," such as "You know?" "OK?" and "You see what I mean?" Talkative persons, of course, engage in much more self-disclosure and use proportionately fewer rhetorical interrogatives.

In studies that have coded actual verbal behavior, it's been observed that there is a major difference in behavior between quiet and talkative persons. Whereas low communication apprehensives communicate in a dominant fashion, attempting to control their dyadic partner, high communication apprehensives (quiet) tend to communicate in an unassertive manner. They seldom disagree and often submit to the assertions and requests of their dyadic partner. We might speculate that this type of communication behavior is related to the high communication apprehensives' low tolerance for disagreement and low assertiveness. In terms of perceptions, Colby, Hopf, and Ayres (1993) in their article on perceptions of communication apprehensives in initial interactions found that when students were paired with partners, with whom they had never met, for a 15-minute initial interaction, high communication apprehensives did not fare as well in the partner-evaluation process as low communication apprehensives. As in other studies, high communication apprehensives were perceived as less attractive, less trustworthy, and less satisfied than low communication apprehensives. Interestingly, high communication apprehensives who interacted saw each other as less socially and task attractive, while low communication apprehensives who interacted saw each other as more socially and task attractive.

Social Settings

Because most social settings involve communicating in dyadic or small groups, it is not surprising that talkative versus quiet persons differ in their behaviors relating to social settings. Although high willing to communicate persons tend to involve themselves in more social activities in general than do low willing to communicate, the most striking differences in their social behaviors relate to dating and marriage.

Research indicates that high and low communicative apprehensives have an equal desire for a social relationship with a member of the opposite sex. Talkative persons, however, report having over twice as many dates in a given time period as do quiet persons. Furthermore, low WTCs report twice the frequency of steady dating reported by high WTCs. Thus, it appears that when a quiet person has a social relationship with a member of the opposite sex, that relationship will be a long-term relationship. On the other hand, outgoing persons appear to "play the field." The strong tendency to engage in exclusive relationships on the part of the quiet person is also evident from her or his behavior with regard to marriage. In a study of college graduates ranging in age from 23 to 64, it was found that over 50% of high communication apprehensives married within a year after completing their undergraduate degree. No similar pattern was found for low communication apprehensives.

At the same time, one's level of communication apprehension with one's dating partner can also have a negative impact on the state of that relationship. In a study by Powers and Love (2000), the researchers found that individuals who had high levels of dating partner communication apprehension (or anxiety associated with communicating with one's dating partner) reported that their dating relationships were not going well: they were not happy with those relationships, they reported lower levels of perceived intimacy, were less likely to continue the relationship, and more likely to view themselves and their dating partners as separate people.

Just as a side note, we should mention that research conducted on dating and marriage relationships has all been what is referred to as heteronormative research. In essence, the research assumes that everyone in the study is heterosexual, so there is no specific research examining whether or not these patterns hold true for lesbian, gay, bisexual, transsexual/transgender, or queer (LGBTQ) romantic relationships. Although there is no specific reason to expect that LGBTQ relationships would function differently, we want to explain the possible limitation to these general findings.

These behavioral patterns suggest that high communication apprehensives find it difficult to establish social relationships and thus make a strong effort to maintain ones they can establish. Low communication apprehensives, on the other hand, find it easier to establish social relationships and, as a result, might be less likely to maintain a relationship that is not completely acceptable to them.

Occupational Choices

The choice of an occupation is one of the most significant choices an individual makes. In large measure, this choice will determine whether the individual will be happy in later life, whether the individual will be successful, and what the economic and social standing of the individual will be. Although many factors influence the choice of an occupation, one of the most important—and possibly the most important—is that individual's level of quietness or willingness to communicate.

Occupations differ greatly in the degree to which they place communication demands on an individual. Consider the differences, for example, between the occupations of biochemist and trial lawyer, between barber and accountant, or between forest ranger and salesperson. We certainly should not be surprised that low WTCs tend to choose occupations with low communication demands, and high WTCs tend to choose occupations with high communication demands. If it were otherwise, the individual might be poorly adjusted, unhappy, and unsuccessful.

We must not overlook an important fact, however. In contemporary industrialized societies, high status and economic reward occupations (with only a few exceptions) are also occupations with high communication demands. In spite of this, the choices people make are those we would expect based on our knowledge of their WTC level (Richmond & Roach, 1992).

One occupation that is clearly communication-based involves sales. A study by Booroom, Goolsby, and Ramsey (1998) found that high CA individuals were less likely to adapt their communication when attempting to sell a product. Furthermore, highly CA individuals were less likely to meet sales quotas and generally earned lower incomes compared with their talkative counterparts. Clearly, sales may not be the best occupational choice for someone who experiences high levels of communication apprehension.

Housing Choices

Where one lives can have a major impact on the amount of communication demanded of that person. Some housing areas place the individual in almost constant contact with others while others provide very little contact.

Housing choices, like occupational choices, are influenced by many factors—not the least of which are cost, location, and availability. Nevertheless, when choosing a place to live, people normally are confronted with several available choices within their financial limitations. Trying to determine the impact that willingness to communicate has on housing choice might seem elusive, yet several conclusions can be drawn from the research on housing choice and its relationship to willingness to communicate.

Quiet persons tend to choose living accommodations that inhibit incidental contact with other people, whereas talkative persons tend to choose accommodations that enhance the possibilities of such contact. For example, in a college dormitory, quiet persons usually prefer to live at the ends of hallways, unless there is a stairway, elevator, or restroom there. These areas tend to be high-interaction areas, so rooms near them are desirable only to talkative persons. Similar variability in degree of area interaction is found in other types of housing, too—in apartment complexes, mobile home parks, or housing developments. Keep in mind that some people select housing areas away from neighbors not because they are high communication apprehensives but simply because they don't desire interaction with neighbors.

Quiet vs. Talkative People: A Generalized Profile

From the behaviors of quiet versus nonquiet persons, we can draw generalized profiles of each. Quiet persons tend to avoid classes that require a lot of interaction and to avoid discussion in small groups; when they do communicate in either situation, they may make irrelevant comments; they sit where interaction demands are lowest, select occupations that require little communication with others, date less than others, marry early, and choose housing in a low-interaction area. Persons more willing to communicate select classes in which interaction will be high; communicate in and perhaps dominate small group discussions; sit where they can control and participate in the communication; select occupations with high communication demands, date often, marry later, and choose housing in a high-interaction area.

Although these profiles are accurate in general, they do not necessarily apply to any single individual with either high or low willingness to communicate. Not every apprehensive person will engage in all of the profiled behaviors of the quiet person, and not every outgoing person will engage in all of the profiled behaviors of the high willingness to communicate individual. Do not assume, therefore, that simply because a person does not take a public speaking course he is not willing to communicate. Only if we observe a person engaging in a large number of the profile

A small group discussion setting is less threatening to most people than is a public-speaking setting.

behaviors are we justified in inferring their level of quietness or anxiety about communicating.

Even so, we recognize that people *do* make assumptions about others based on their communicative behavior. The remainder of this chapter reviews how quiet people and talkative people are perceived by others and the impact these perceptions can have on interpersonal relations in everyday life.

As you read the next section, keep in mind that (1) communication apprehension is a cognitive feeling of anxiety or fear, while (2) shyness is the behavior of being quiet or withdrawing from communication situations, and (3) willingness to communicate is the desire, or attitude, or inclination to talk with others. We will examine the impact that CA, shyness, and willingness to communicate has in different situations. For reading ease, in many instances we will simply refer to the shy person as quiet versus the nonshy person who is verbal, talkative, or outgoing.

Interpersonal Perceptions

Verbal behavior is extremely important in the development of interpersonal relationships and perceptions. As noted earlier, in general, the more a person talks the more positively that person will be perceived, unless the content of what is said is offensive. In the beginning of an interpersonal relationship, sometimes referred to as the "acquaintance stage" of the relationship, the impact of verbal behavior is vital. Since the two people do not know one another, they are uncertain how to react to one another. Uncertainty usually can be reduced only by looking, listening, and exchanging information (talking). If one person chooses not to talk or to talk very little, the other remains uncertain about how to relate to that person. Frequently in such situations the partner of the quiet person simply chooses to terminate the relationship, which is the line of least resistance.

Uncertainty makes most people uncomfortable. We tend to make an effort to resolve the uncertainty. In most instances people must talk to learn more about each other. Those who do not talk enough do not only fail to eliminate their own uncertainty, but also might be perceived in a less positive manner by others. Shy people, because of their tendency to avoid communication, tend to produce negative perceptions in the minds of others. Talkative people, because of their desire for communication, tend to produce positive perceptions in others. Although these differential perceptions might be altered as people get better acquainted, relationships are often terminated because of initial negative perceptions before the time needed to know one another has passed.

So far, we have considered only general perceptions. At this point, we will consider specific perceptions and how other people perceive quiet versus verbal persons. Since the research on communication apprehension, shyness, and willingness to communicate generated the same results, we will refer to high communication apprehensives as quiet people and low communication apprehensives as talkative people. By changing the terminology at this point, we hope to emphasize the fact that it is differences in communication behavior and inclination to talk or not talk that generate differences in perceptions, not just differences in apprehension levels. Whether the differences in communication behavior are produced by communication apprehension or by such variables as willingness to communicate, skill deficiencies, social introversion, cultural divergence, or alienation, the differential communication behaviors will result in differential perception of quiet versus talkative people.

Competence

In U.S. culture and several other cultures where research was conducted, it was found that people have a stereotype of quiet people as being less competent and less intelligent than talkative people. It is important that we recognize that this is a stereotype, not a factually based observation. Several researchers have attempted to demonstrate that there is a positive relationship between intelligence and the amount a person talks, but no meaningful relationship has been found. Nevertheless, quiet people are often perceived as less competent and less intelligent than their counterparts. Such perceptions have been demonstrated in interpersonal and small-group contexts as well as in work and in school environments.

Although these perceptions are based on faulty stereotypes, it should be recognized that such perceptions can sometimes lead to self-fulfilling prophecies. In elementary schools, for example, it has been demonstrated that if teachers expect a child to do well, it is increasingly likely the child will do well. The reverse is also true. To some extent, then, we become what others perceive and expect us to be (see Appendix J).

Despite the fact that there is no relationship between talkativeness and competence in general, there is one exception to this rule. That is in the area of communication competence. Talkative people are perceived to be more communicatively competent, and the perception is generally an accurate one. Quiet people accept fewer opportunities to practice their communication skills and to the extent practice helps improve skill, their communication skills might be less developed. In contrast, talkative people look for opportunities to practice and refine their communication skills.

Anxiety

Quiet people are perceived to be more anxious about communication than talkative people. Unlike the perceptions concerning intelligence and general competence, these perceptions frequently are accurate. Although not all quiet people are apprehensive about communication, a large proportion are, which causes others to stereotype all quiet people—a stereotype that is shared even by quiet people themselves when reporting their perceptions of other quiet people. Quiet people are also perceived to be less extroverted and less composed. Such perceptions are more likely to be accurate than inaccurate, but again, this does not mean we can generalize.

Sociocommunicative Style

Sociocommunicative style refers to the way a person is perceived in her or his relations with other people. There are two primary dimensions of sociocommunicative style: assertiveness and responsiveness (see Chapter 6 for more discussion). Assertiveness refers to a person's ability to state opinions with conviction and to be able to defend one's opinions and oneself. Responsiveness refers to a person's willingness to be responsive or open to another during interpersonal interaction (see Appendix O).

Quiet people are perceived to be lower in assertiveness and responsiveness, and talkative people are perceived to be higher in both. These perceptions appear to be accurate. Research indicates that over half of the people identified as low in assertiveness and responsiveness are high communication apprehensives. In addition, 70% of the people identified as high communication apprehensives have been found to be low in assertiveness and responsiveness. In short, quiet people are accurately perceived as those who have difficulty expressing their opinions to others with conviction and responding to others in an open and sensitive way. Talkative people generally are perceived in an opposite manner.

Leadership

Talkative people are more likely to be perceived as leaders than quiet people. To function as a leader in most situations requires at least a moderate degree of communication with other people. Thus, it is not surprising that people who do not talk much are not perceived to function as leaders. The perception is correct more often than not.

It is interesting to note, however, that in some instances relatively quiet people can function as leaders to some degree. For example, the information they provide can change the course of a group discussion and alter the ultimate decision of the group. Yet even in such an instance, the quiet person is not perceived by group members as the leader. In fact, several research studies have found that when good ideas come from a quiet person within a group, the group tends to report that the information came from a more talkative group member when the group is questioned about people's ideas at a later point. The reason for this conclusion is the talkative person picks up on the idea introduced by the quiet person and runs with it, while the quiet person sits quietly by and watches.

Another type of leadership, opinion leadership, is also important to consider. An opinion leader is someone to whom we turn for information or advice when we need to make a decision. Talkative people are much more likely to be perceived as opinion leaders than quiet people. Again, the perception is probably accurate in most cases than not. Quiet people are unlikely to go out of their way to offer opinions, and since they are perceived by others as less competent, they are less likely to be asked for their opinions concerning an issue or a decision.

Attractiveness

Quiet people are perceived to be less sociable and friendly than are talkative people. As we noted previously, communication is a vital element in reducing uncertainty in human relationships. Consequently, a reduced level of communication appears to be interpreted by most people as a sign of unfriendliness. Not surprisingly, therefore, quiet people are perceived as less attractive than are talkative people. It is interesting to note this perception is held not only by more talkative people but also by quiet people themselves, who not only see other quiet people as unattractive, but also view themselves as less attractive than more talkative people.

From these perceptions we have outlined, you can draw perceptual profiles of the quiet and talkative person. The quiet person is perceived to be less competent, less communicatively competent, more anxious about communication, less composed and extroverted, less assertive and responsive, either not a leader or an opinion leader, less sociable and friendly, and less attractive. The talkative person is perceived to be more competent in general, more communicatively competent, less anxious about communication, more composed and extroverted, more assertive and responsive, a leader and an opinion leader, more friendly and sociable, and more attractive.

Some of these perceptions are probably accurate in many instances; others are overgeneralized, stereotypical perceptions. Whether right or wrong, however, the perceptions exist and have a direct impact on the everyday lives of talkative and quiet people.

Everyday Life

People do not react to us as we are; they react to us as they perceive us to be. We may be more competent than the people around us, but if others perceive us to be less competent, we will be treated as less competent. This is a fact of life in human relationships, whether we like it or not. Relationships are built on perceptions, not reality. Perceptions are based in a large part on communication behavior. We have already noted the common impact on perception of the communication behaviors of quiet and talkative people. At this point, we turn to the impact of these perceptions on three important aspects of everyday life: interpersonal relationships, school environment, organizational environment, health care, and online.

Peer Relationships

As we noted previously, people who are quiet are perceived as less friendly and attractive than more talkative people. It is not surprising, therefore, that quiet people tend to have problems in the social environment. We already noted that quiet people have far fewer dates than talkative people. They also have far fewer people they can call "friends," less than half as many as their more talkative peers.

Social relationships require a certain degree of communication between people to be established and maintained. If someone doesn't want to talk to us, it is natural for us to simply disregard that person and move onto someone else. Visualize, if you can, a very quiet person in a singles bar or at a cocktail party. How many new people do you think he or she will meet? Now contrast this by visualizing a talkative person in the same setting.

In a study of over 400 college students, quiet and talkative students were asked to indicate how many people they knew whom they would classify as "good friends." Responses ranged from none to over 20. Of particular interest is the fact that over a third of the quiet people reported having no good friends at all, while not a single talkative person reported having no good friends. When asked to list the names of their good friends, over half of those named by the quiet persons were relatives such as parents, siblings, or cousins. Less than 5% of the talkative persons mentioned any relatives in this category.

The social environment requires effective communication for the establishment of good relationships. Quiet people tend to fare less well in the social environment than do talkative persons.

Family Relationships

As with peer relationships, people who are quiet tend to have different familial interactions than more talkative people. In the family communication literature, we typically talk about two primary types of family communication patterns: conversation orientation and conformity orientation. A conversation-oriented family is a family that emphasizes the open expression of ideas and encourages family members to challenge one another's arguments in an open debate. On the other hand, a conformity-oriented family is one where the emphasis is on creating harmonious relationships with one's parents. In conformity-oriented families, children are taught early on that disagreeing with one's parents is simply not tolerated, so children simply internalize their disagreements to avoid disharmony.

In a study by Hsu (1998), a positive relationship between conformity orientation and communication apprehension was found, and a negative relationship was found between conversation orientation and communication apprehension. Furthermore, CA was found to negatively relate to perceptions of family cohesion, family expressiveness, and family independence. Clearly, how an individual's family communicates at home can have an impact on both group and interpersonal contexts (the most closely related to the types of interactions an individual engages in within her or his family).

Other research has examined how a child's communication apprehension with his parent has an impact on the nature of that relationship. Lucchetti, Powers, and Love (2002) found that children who were communicatively apprehensive when talking with their parents reported lower levels of relationship satisfaction.

School Environment

As we have noted, people who are quiet are perceived to be less competent and less intelligent than more talkative people. Such perceptions have a direct impact in a school environment. Although there is at least some positive impact (quiet children are less likely to get into trouble with the teacher), most of the impact is negative. In general, teachers expect quiet children to do less well in school and, as a result, might treat the quiet child as if he or she were less intelligent. The quiet child is less likely to be called upon to respond in class and thus has less opportunity to correct learning mistakes. The quiet child receives less attention from the teacher and thus less reinforcement when he or she does something well. Because of their desire to avoid communication with their teachers, quiet children also ask for assistance less frequently and volunteer to participate less, thus having less opportunity to learn and be positively reinforced. Although this impact is present in education at all levels, it is most severe in elementary grades. Because quiet children often are incorrectly perceived as poor readers or lazy students, they are placed in "slow" groups. Many are never able to overcome this poor start, and they become what they were incorrectly perceived as being: the slow student.

Because many courses are graded at least partially on participation, quiet people often receive lower grades than their more talkative peers, even though their achievement might actually be equal or even superior to that of their peers. In a very real sense, quiet people are discriminated against in the school environment. The impact of this discrimination is cumulative over the years of schooling. Consequently, by the time young people complete high school, their learning, as measured by standardized achievement tests, is affected. Even though there is no meaningful difference in intelligence, quiet children on average score lower on precollege achievement tests than do their talkative peers. In fact, in an examining of multiple studies conducting by Bourhis, Allen, and Bauman (2006), the researchers found that students with higher levels of communication apprehension had lower measures of intelligence, lower grade-point averages, lower grades in particular courses, and lower grades on individual assignments as compared with their lower-CA peers. Furthermore, this trend was consistent across different types of courses, which included math, English, and reading. Finally, these negative associations were similar in children in elementary school and young adults in college. So, it's not surprising, then, that some research has revealed that the quiet college student is substantially below the talkative college student in grade-point average at the end of the first year of college. Although quiet children tend to achieve less than their aptitudes would justify, talkative children may achieve at a level above what their aptitudes would justify. Because of their willingness to engage in communication with their teachers and their peers, their opportunities for learning and reinforcement are increased. The ultimate effect of talkativeness, then, is increased learning and self-confidence. One interesting caveat to this general narrative was noted in a study by Butler, Proyr, and Marti (2004) who examined CA levels between honors and non-honors students in a university. Overall, the researchers found that honors students actually had higher levels of CA when compared with their non-honors peers. Clearly, highly CA individuals can be high academic achieving individuals.

Recent research has also revealed that the quiet child's peers perceive the quiet child as being less approachable, less friendly, and less intelligent than the talkative child. This perception begins as early as the third grade and remains throughout the high-school levels. As McCroskey and Richmond (2006) note, highly CA students end up with a highly restricted social life as a result of their CA. High CA students end up talking to their peers and teachers less. Stockstill and Roach (2007) surveyed 2,553 high school students and found that student athletes generally had lower levels of communication apprehension when compared with nonstudent athletes. In essence, high CA students are less likely to participate in extracurricular activities.

Differential attitudes and behaviors related to communication not only affect students, but they also affect teachers. Research indicates quiet teachers are not liked as well by their students as talkative teachers. This has an impact not only on the way teachers are evaluated but also on their effectiveness. Students are less inclined to follow the recommendations of quiet teachers than they are to follow the recommendations of more talkative ones. Research suggests that quiet teachers, particularly those who are high communication apprehensives, are sensitive to the fact students might respond negatively to them. They overwhelmingly choose to teach in the lower elementary grades. They report they are less afraid to communicate with the younger children than they would be to communicate with children in the upper grades, junior high, or in high school. Whether these teachers are more effective with little children than they would be with older children is not yet known.

Further research by Malachowski, Martin, and Vallade (2013) found that individuals with high CA levels differ with respect to how they respond to teacher feedback in the classroom. Students with high levels of CA were more sensitive to receiving feedback, preferred to receive feedback privately, and did not find feedback to be overly useful. Talkaholics, on the other hand, did not differ in their perceptions of instructor feedback at all. This is just another example of how a student's level of CA can have an impact on her or his classroom experience.

In summary, the school environment requires effective communication on the part of both students and teachers. Quiet people tend to fare less well in the school environment than talkative people.

Work Environment

As noted previously, people who are quiet are perceived to be less competent, less likely to be leaders, less assertive and responsive, and less attractive than more talkative people. The impact of these perceptions may be felt most strongly in the work environment (Richmond & Roach, 1992).

Since quiet people tend to choose occupations with low communication requirements, and talkative people tend to choose occupations with higher communication requirements, we might assume the impact of their differential communication behaviors would be negated in this environment. Such is not the case.

To begin with, quiet people are less likely to be offered an interview for a position than are talkative people. To be referred to as "quiet" or "reticent" in a recommendation for a job is almost the kiss of death. With other qualifications being equal, another applicant will be given the interview. In fact, even if other qualifications are not equal, this is likely to be the outcome.

Once an interview is obtained, the road to employment does not become smooth for quiet persons. Their communication behavior in the interview is most likely to generate negative perceptions of the types we discussed previously. The talkative person, on the other hand, is likely to make a good impression in the interview, particularly if he does not over-communicate.

This does not necessarily indicate that quiet people do not obtain jobs or that the thousands of people on our unemployment rolls are all quiet people. Quiet people do obtain employment, but the positions they obtain typically provide lower status and pay than positions obtained by more talkative people. This is partially a function of the quiet person seeking a position with low communication demands, and such positions generally are lower status, lower paying positions. It is also, however, partly a function of an employer's unwillingness to hire a quiet person for a better position in the organization.

Once employed, quiet people and talkative people are not equally successful. Research in a variety of occupations indicates quiet people report lower job satisfaction than the average employee, while talkative people report higher than average satisfaction. In many instances, actual job performance quality differs as well. For example, talkative people are far more successful in sales and administrative positions, as would be expected. Quiet people fare somewhat better in routine, nonsupervisory positions. When it comes time for a promotion, the difference between quiet people and talkative people becomes most dramatic. Research indicates that not only are quiet people not promoted frequently, but also they usually do not anticipate being promoted or even want to be promoted. Most promotions require increased communicative responsibilities involving supervision, and everyone sees the quiet person as a poor candidate for such a position, including the quiet person. Talkative persons, on the other hand, are prime candidates for promotion and tend to populate the upper levels of most organizations. For these reasons, research has found that people that are high CA in the organization tend to be on the lower rungs of the hierarchy and make less money than their talkative counterparts.

High CA individuals also appear to be at a disadvantage in terms of the types and amount of information they need to have to complete their jobs. In a study conducted by Bartoo and Sias (2004), the researchers set out to determine if high CA subordinates were receiving enough information on the job to complete assigned tasks and whether high CA supervisors were providing enough information to their subordinates. Overall, the researchers found that an individual's CA did not appear to have an impact on the type of information they received. However, a supervisor's level of communication apprehension has a negative impact on the amount of information they provided their subordinates related to both information subordinates need to complete a task and information about the organization as a whole. Ultimately, subordinates with high CA supervisors reported what is called information underload, that is, not having enough information. High CA subordinates, on the other hand, believed they were receiving too much information or were experiencing information overload.

Finally, it has been found that quiet people tend to retain positions with the same organization for shorter periods than do talkative people. In one investigation, for example, talkative people were found to have 50% more seniority than quiet people. This might seem unusual. But when employers have to make "cutbacks," they would rather let the quiet person go than the talkative person. The quiet person will usually go quietly, the talkative person won't leave quietly. In fact, they might even initiate a lawsuit against the organization.

Despite the communication challenges that quiet people clearly have in the modern workplaces, quiet people often make it into positions of leadership. Even in leadership positions quiet people still have many hurdles to overcome. Cole and McCroskey (2003) examined subordinate perceptions of their supervisor's levels of communication apprehension and various other attributes. Subordinates who perceived their supervisors as high CA believed those supervisors were more verbally aggressive, less competent, were less likely to care about the subordinate or show the subordinate goodwill, and less trustworthy. Overall, subordinates who viewed their supervisors as communicatively apprehensive had more negative attitudes toward those supervisors and simply did not like those supervisors.

As you can see, the work environment requires effective communication to obtain and retain employment. Quiet people tend to fall into a "last to be hired, last to be promoted, first to be fired" pattern similar to that of several minority groups against whom systematic discrimination has been practiced. Talkative people find it easier to obtain quality employment, tend to be successful in their work, and are likely to be retained and promoted.

From the effects we have outlined above, we can, once again, draw profiles of the quiet person and the talkative person. The talkative person is more likely to be successful in the school environment, to establish good social relationships, and to be successful in the world of work. The quiet person is less likely to be successful in school, has difficulty establishing interpersonal relationships, and has difficulty obtaining and retaining employment.

Health Care

Although we know that prolonged anxiety causes all kinds of negative physiological outcomes (e.g., high blood pressure, ulcers, irritable bowel syndrome, erectile dysfunction, fatigue, nausea, headaches, etc.), very little research has actually been conducted to examine communication apprehension's relationship to one's health. Wheeless (1984) conducted the first study examining the effect that communication apprehension has on health care. In this study, Wheeless examined the relationship between an individual's communication apprehension and her likelihood of discussing various gynecological issues (i.e., use of contraceptives, heavy menstrual bleeding, pain occurring during intercourse, etc.) with her gynecologist. Overall, Wheeless found that individuals with high levels of CA were less likely to discuss the whole range of gynecological problems with their gynecologists. Obviously, if someone is unwilling to discuss serious medical issues with her gynecologist, this lack of information could lead to negative medical outcomes.

In 1998, Richmond, Smith, Heisel, and McCroskey created the Fear of Physician (FOP) scale as a general tool to assess one's level of CA with one's physician (see Appendix P). This measure was designed to assess specific levels of apprehension with one's physician and not just CA as a general concept. In their initial study, the researchers found that individuals who fear talking with their physicians generally reported less satisfaction with their medical care and less satisfaction with their physicians in general. In a 2001 follow-up study, Richmond et al. once again found that fear of talking with one's physician was negatively related to perceived quality of

Quiet persons tend to avoid classes that require a lot of interaction and to avoid discussion in small groups.

medical care, but the researchers also reported that individuals who feared talking with their physicians also believed their physicians were not non-verbally immediate. As discussed earlier in this book, nonverbal imme-diacy is important in creating close, intimate interactions with others. In a more recent study examining FOP in an international setting, Hashemi, Hadavi, and Valinejad (2016) found that patient FOP was detrimental to effective patient–physician interactions in Rafsanjan, Iran. This type of international replication is important because it demonstrates the simi-larity of impact that these variables have in both the United States and in other countries.

In a study by Booth-Butterfield, Chory, and Beynon (1997), the researchers were interested in how one's level of CA had an impact on health behaviors (using tobacco, exercising, dieting, speaking with med-ical representatives at health fairs, etc.) and how CA had an impact on medical interviews. First, there was no relationship between CA and using tobacco, exercising, or dieting. Not surprisingly, high CA individuals were less likely to speak to medical representatives at health fairs. Second, CA in this study was shown to have a negative impact on the medical interview. In essence, high CA individuals reported that they were less likely to ask their physician questions, less likely to understand their physicians, less likely to feel understood by their physicians, and more likely to end the patient-physician encounter quickly.

One experimental study manipulated physician biographies to see if perceived similarity could impact people with CA's perceptions of phy-sicians (Perrault & Silk, 2015). Overall, the study found that perceived similarity with a physician based on reading her or his biography led to greater uncertainty reduction, greater liking, and subsequent reductions in CA with the physician for high CA participants. Practically speaking, health practitioners could help alleviate some of their patients' CA simply by having an engaging and well-rounded biography that the patients could read prior to their first visit. It's sometimes these simple touches that really can help alleviate anxiety.

One factor of health communication that often has people at a loss for words involves death. Eventually, everyone is going to do, but talking about death and dying can cause many people to be anxious. Carmack and DeGroot (2016) set out to examine this phenomenon. The researchers ultimately broke CA about dying into two different categories: anxiety and avoidance. First, the researchers found that an individual's general level of communication apprehension was positively related to both anxiety and avoidance of communication about death. Second, the researchers found that individuals who experienced high levels of CA about death (both anxiety and avoidance) were more likely to be afraid of their own deaths and the deaths of others. These results definitely have huge implications for medical personnel when it comes to discussing end-of-life decision-making.

Overall, an individual's level CA clearly has an impact on how he or she functions with regards to her or his health. As such, high CA individuals are less likely to communicate important symptoms to their physicians and will ultimately end up with more health problems because of the lack of communication.

Online

From Internet chatting to instant messaging, e-mailing, using social media sites, and texting, modern mediated technologies are reshaping the ways in which people communicate on a daily basis. One of the biggest problems researchers have faced examining communication in these changing technologies has been the speed at which the technologies change. For example, a researcher may start out examining CA in a specific technology only to have that specific technology become antiquated by the time the research is actually published. As such, this section is going to focus less on how CA has been examined in various technologies and look more at some of the general findings of CA across various technologies.

First, research consistently shows us that these technologies are generally viewed as new forms of communication. As such, people who are highly talkative are more likely to adopt and regularly use various forms of computer-mediated communication (CMC) technologies than people who are quiet. Some researchers originally suspected that because these communication modalities didn't involve face-to-face (FtF) interactions, high CA individuals would flock to them as an alternative. Although there was some flocking during the early days of Internet relay chatting (early to mid-1990s), this flocking generally stopped as the technologies became more mainstream.

Second, time spent utilizing and developing one's skills with different CMC technologies generally helps alleviate communication apprehension with a specific technology. As Wrench and Punyanunt-Carter (2007) noted, the more people spend using a CMC technology the more comfortable they will become communicating using the technology and the more communicatively competent they will become using the technology. As a result of this comfort, they start to view these interactions as more and more like FtF interactions, which will lead to healthy and productive CMC interactions. Wrench and Punyanunt-Carter (2007) specifically focused on three technologies within this study: instant messaging apprehension, chatting apprehension, and e-mail apprehension (see Appendix Q for this measure), and all three were negatively related both with perceived skill and perceived communication competence.

In a study by Cortese and Seo (2012), the researchers set out to examine how an individual's level of communication apprehension affects their view of interacting with others. One common theory in CMC, social presence theory, attempts to explain why people perceive interactions in an online environment as real or not. In essence, people who experience presence see their interactions online as similar to their interactions offline, while people who do not experience presence see their interactions as disjointed and fake. In Cortese and Seo's study, the researchers found that individuals with high levels of CA were less likely to experience social presence in their online interactions.

In study by Punyanunt-Carter, De La Cruz, and Wrench (2017) the authors examined the impact that CA has on social media use (and Snapchat specifically). The authors found that individuals with higher levels of CA were less likely to utilize Snapchat for relational purposes, but they were likely to use Snapchat for functional purposes, which was the same pattern that was found for overall social media use in the study.

Basically, most people today use CMC as a supplement to FtF interactions and not a substitute for FtF interactions. During the early days of the Internet, people who utilized CMC technologies were widely dispersed, so the majority of these early interactions happened with people at large geographic distances. Today, most of our CMC interactions are not with people around the world but with people we sit with in class, our families, and our friends. Because CMC has become so normalized in our world, more people are using this technology to enhance their FtF relationships and not as a substitute for their FtF relationships. It should be no surprise, then, that high CA people are less likely to utilize this technology because it is viewed today as an extension of FtF interactions.

Krishnan and Atkin (2014) examined individual use of social networking sites (SNSs; Facebook, Twitter, Instagram, etc.) to see if it differed based on an individual's level of communication apprehension. The authors found that individuals who were already proficient in social and face-to-face (FtF) communication behaviors, were more likely to utilize social networking sites than those who were not. Basically, individuals with lower levels of CA see SNSs as another tool for communication, which still provokes anxiety, so they are less likely to use the technology. On the other hand, individuals who have low levels of CA see SNSs as another tool for interacting with others, so they readily welcome these new tools into their communication toolbelt.

In another study conducted by Hammick and Lee (2014), the researchers set out to determine if individuals with various shyness levels would respond differently to online discussions compared to FtF discussions. Participants were either placed into a virtual discussion group that used simulated avatars or in a face-to-face discussion group. Shy individuals reported less CA in the virtual discussion as compared to the FtF discussions. Non-shy individuals did not differ in their levels of CA in either environment. In essence, virtual environments can help individuals who are shy decrease their levels of CA when interacting with other people.

Overall, computer-mediated communication apprehension (CMCA) is a distinct form of communication apprehension and just another context of communication apprehension. For individuals who have state levels of CA, they will experience some anxiety when they start interacting with people using this new technology. These state-level individuals will see a decrease in their communication apprehension over time as they become more technologically savvy and build new interaction skills. However, people who have trait-levels of CA are still going to experience high levels of CA, they just now have a new medium through which their anxiety is realized.

Conclusion

Most quiet people consider their quietness to be a problem. Most talkative people do not consider their talkativeness to be a problem. As a result, most communication research has been directed toward the problems associated with quietness. Much of this work has been directed toward devising ways of helping quiet people. Some of these methods are outlined in Chapter 7. Before we look at these methods, however, in Chapter 6 we'll review how apprehension and shyness impact communication effectiveness.

DISCUSSION QUESTIONS

1. In relationships, why does uncertainty make most people uncomfortable? How can uncertainty in relationships be overcome?
2. "The more a person talks, in most cases, the more positively they will be perceived." Why is this statement generally true?
3. What instance(s) can cause a talkative person to be perceived in a negative manner by others?
4. Why are quiet people perceived as less competent, more anxious, less assertive, and less responsive than talkative persons?
5. How is talkativeness versus quietness related to leadership and opinion leadership?
6. "People do not react to us as we are, they react to us as they perceive us to be." Is this statement true? If true, why? If false, why?
7. The literature indicates that a person's level of quietness or talkativeness has an impact on perceptions in everyday life. What are the specific impacts on the school environment, the social environment, and the work environment?
8. What are the general profiles of the quiet person versus the talkative person?
9. Are all talkative persons happy and well-adjusted models to emulate? Justify your answer.
10. Are all quiet persons in our environment poor, unfortunate souls who should be pitied? Justify your answer.

ACTIVITIES

1. Spend one entire day being quiet (noncommunicative) with your friends, family, teachers, employers, or whomever you come into contact with most frequently. Keep a record of others' responses to your quietness. Record any comments people make and any reactions they have.
2. Obtain access to an organization and observe where the talkative, outgoing persons are employed. Look at the communication demands they have to handle on a daily basis. In addition, record how many outgoing, talkative persons have others (such as secretaries) to handle much of the company communication for them so they can direct their communication to their supervisors.
3. Write the job recommendation for yourself that you would like— your immediate supervisor or a friend or colleague to write about you. Emphasize your positive communication skills, communication

competencies, and communication qualifications. Have a colleague or teacher read your recommendation to see where improvements might be made. Remember, a significant part of obtaining a good position is being able to sell yourself based on your potential to be an effective communicator.

4. Venture into a new communication technology that you are not as familiar with right now (e.g., Social Networking Site, World of Warcraft, Yahoo! Chatrooms, etc.). Try to interact with people from your own country and then with people from a different country. How do you see your own sense of computer-mediated communication apprehension affecting you differently in both contexts? Try having multiple types of interactions across different platforms and keep track of your interactions in a journal.

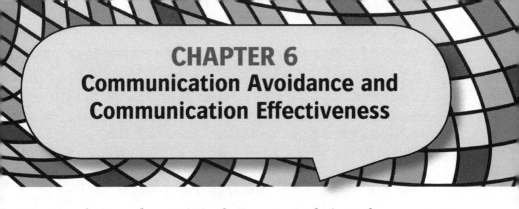

CHAPTER 6
Communication Avoidance and Communication Effectiveness

Most people in modem societies have a strong desire to be competent communicators. Although communication scholars are far from being in agreement as to what actually constitutes "communication competence," nonscholars are nearly unanimous in agreeing that to be competent is to be an effective communicator; in other words, to accomplish one's purposes through communication in a socially appropriate manner.

Exactly what it takes to be an effective communicator has been the subject of countless research efforts and thousands of published articles and books. In fact, the oldest essay ever discovered, written about 3000 B.C., consists of advice on how to speak effectively. This essay was inscribed on a fragment of parchment addressed to Kagetnni, the eldest son of the Pharaoh Huni. Similarly, the oldest extant book is a treatise on effective communication. This book, known as the Precepts, was written in Egypt about 2675 B.C. by Ptah-Hotep for the use of the pharaoh's son. Some of the greatest scholars of antiquity, including Plato, Aristotle, and Cicero, focused much of their attention on what constitutes effective communication. Thus, our understanding of communication is drawn from nearly 5,000 years of contributions from some of the greatest scholars in history, and this concern with determining the various aspects of communication effectiveness has continued to the present (McCroskey, Wrench, and Richmond, 2003).

With all of this concern and effort, you might think we would now know exactly what it takes to be an effective communicator in any given situation. Unfortunately, this is not the case. Given the number of possible communicators, topics, and contexts, an almost infinite number of possible communication situations exist. Thus, being able to determine precisely what will make a communicator effective in every possible situation probably is beyond human potential. We can, however, suggest that communication competence is the "adequate ability to pass along or give information; the ability to make known by talking or writing" (McCroskey & McCroskey, 1986, p. 1). In addition, there are two ways to determine competence. The first asks individuals to self-report their perceptions of their communication competence (self-perceived communication competence). The second approach looks at what individuals predict their behavior responses would be in situations (social style of individuals and immediacy behaviors). Each of these approaches will be reviewed and the outcomes discussed. First, however, we outline some of the elements that appear to be important contributors to effectiveness regardless of the situation.

Contributors to Communication Effectiveness

Three major elements appear to have the most impact on the development of effective communication: behavioral skills; cognitive skills; and affective orientations toward communication. We will consider each in turn.

Behavioral Skills

Certain communication skills are essential to effective communication. Most of these are obvious, and some receive considerable attention in modern educational systems. Such variables are language acquisitions in the culture in which one lives, learning appropriate articulation skills, and overcoming social communication disorders (dyssemia, pragmatic disorders, stuttering, verbal impairment, and so on) are critical. Other skills such as typing, telephone usage, and use of a word processor can also be vitally important, although not as central as the previously mentioned skills.

Skills such as the ones noted are essentially behavioral in nature. They are the foundation upon which effective communication can be built. Some are formally taught in schools, while others are learned primarily through association with parents or from one's culture. Although there is much room for improvement in the handling of these skills by our educational systems, a remarkably high percentage of people do develop at least adequate levels of these skills by the time they reach adulthood. Unfortunately, acquisition of communication skills is only a step toward becoming an effective communicator, not a guarantee an individual will become one.

Cognitive Skills

Cognitive skills are central to becoming truly effective in communication. Such skills involve understanding the communication process and being able to make appropriate choices of what to communicate and, depending on the context and situation, what not to communicate. Some of the most basic and important cognitive skills are developing an understanding of how differently words are used by each individual, how nonverbal messages are used in one's culture, when it is appropriate and beneficial to assert oneself, and how one may communicate friendliness to another. This list of cognitive skills that can assist one in becoming a more effective communicator is far from complete, of course, but it is illustrative of the types of skills that are important. Cognitive skills are often taught in introduction to communication courses or discussed in introductory to communication books like our book *Human Communication in Everyday Life: Explanations and Applications* (Wrench et al., 2008).

As was the case with behavioral skills, cognitive communication skills can be learned through formal instruction in the schools and/or through experience in communication with other people in one's culture. The latter method is essentially trial and error, and it provides no guarantee one will learn the appropriate information. Formal instruction in the cognitive skills related to communication effectiveness is limited in most of our school systems, including our colleges and universities. Most formal instruction focuses on behavioral skills, and in many schools no formal instruction related to the cognitive aspect of communication is available at all. It should not be surprising, therefore, that the overwhelming majority of people in modern society are not communicatively competent.

Affective Orientations

The final element critical to the development of communication competence is the individual's affective orientations toward communication. By this we mean the person's feelings about and attitudes toward communication.

All of the behavioral and cognitive skills in the world will not make a person an effective communicator if they do not want to be one. A person has to want to be an effective communicator and care whether he or she is effective in order to actually be effective. There must be a desire in the individual to influence others, or the person simply is not likely to be motivated to use whatever behavioral and cognitive skills he or she has. This desire must be coupled with the requisite communication skills; of course, desire alone does not make one an effective communicator.

In this chapter, we discuss the other critical affective orientation toward communication: communication apprehension. People who are afraid to communicate are unlikely to be effective communicators. As we note, if one is afraid to communicate, no amount of behavioral or cognitive skill will make that person an effective communicator. On the other hand, just because a person is not apprehensive about communication does not mean the person will be effective. Lower levels of communication apprehension will simply allow the individual to use whatever skills he possesses, it will not magically produce new skills. Because communication apprehension serves as such a strong inhibitor, many people believe it is the single most significant barrier to effective communication in modem society.

We should mention that some individuals do suffer from real communication disorders that make it difficult for them to acquire specific behavioral/cognitive skills or affective orientations. For example, autistic children often have problems enacting and understanding/interpreting nonverbal behavior from others. As such, there is an entire field of specialists in communication disorders who help individuals and their families cope with these more severe diagnoses.

In the following sections, we consider components that we believe are central to effective communication and discuss how communication apprehension and a low willingness to communicate tend to reduce the probability that an individual will use these. We focus on the constructs of self-perceived communication competence, social style, and immediacy.

Self-Perceived Communication Competence

It is often stated that the best way to find out something about someone is to simply ask her or him. This is probably true in the case of feelings of communication competence. McCroskey and McCroskey (1986) developed the Self-Perceived Communication Competence scale (SPCC, see Appendix J). The SPCC is composed of 12 items that were chosen to reflect four basic communication contexts: (1) public speaking; (2) talking in a large meeting; (3) talking in a small group; and (4) talking in a dyad, and three common types of receivers: (1) strangers; (2) acquaintances; and (3) friends. For each combination of context and receiver type, people are asked to estimate their communication competence on a 0 to 100 scale. In addition to a global self-perceived communication competence score, the scale permits generating subscores for each type of communication context and receiver.

Studies by McCroskey and his associates indicate that total SPCC scores have been found to correlate positively with self-esteem, willingness to communicate, general attitude toward communication, argumentativeness, and sociability. Similarly, significant negative correlations have been found with communication apprehension, alienation, anomia, neuroticism, introversion, and shyness. These results suggest that personality substantially affects an individual's perception of her or his communication competence. The strong correlation with willingness to communicate also suggests the potential of the meaningful impact of self-perceived communication competence on actual communication behavior. For example, the higher one perceives her or his competence to be effective with strangers, the more likely he or she will approach strangers and communicate with them. Similarly, the negative correlation between CA and SPCC suggests that the higher the apprehension, the lower the self-perceived communication competence.

It is important to recognize that how competent a person believes herself or himself to be is not necessarily related to how competently the person will communicate in any given situation. We have all met buffoons who are incompetent but think the opposite. Nevertheless, how competent a person thinks he or she is very much associated with the person's desire to communicate. Hence, self-perceived competence in many cases might be more important than actual, behavioral competence.

Sociocommunicative Style

Effective interpersonal communicators exhibit three important elements in their communication: assertiveness, responsiveness, and versatility. Research points to the centrality of these three elements. The most significant research was initiated by Dr. David W. Merrill in 1966 when he was president of Personnel Predictions and Research, Inc. (Personnel Predictions and Research, Inc., became part of The TRACOM Corporation in 1978; Merrill & Reid, 1981; Newton, 1986). This research has produced an immense body of data concerning interpersonal effectiveness under the label of "social style." Others, such as William B. Lashbrook and his colleagues at Wilson Learning Corporation, have also studied sociommunicative style. Still others have studied similar concepts under the label of "androgyny" or "psychological gender." These bodies of literature appeared to be totally independent until recently, as researchers have measured remarkably similar constructs and drawn conclusions about communication effectiveness that are also very similar. We will consider each of the three central elements below.

Assertiveness

Assertiveness is the capacity to make requests; to actively disagree; to express positive or negative personal rights and feelings; to initiate, maintain, or disengage from conversations; and to stand up for one's self without attacking another. In some research, this aspect of communication is stereotyped as "masculinity." Of course, such communication behavior is not exclusively performed by males, yet in U.S. culture the stereotype of appropriate male behavior in communication is closely associated with this characteristic. A scale related to assertiveness and responsiveness (based on the works of Bem, 1974; Merrill & Reid, 1981; Wheeless & Dierks-Stewart, 1981) is included in Appendix O. When you examine the measure, note that such things as "defends own beliefs," "acts as a leader," "dominant," and "willing to take a stand" are associated with the assertiveness construct. Although such terms do describe the stereotyped male image in U.S. society, they more importantly describe a person who is in control of himself and his communication.

It is important to distinguish between assertiveness and aggressiveness, since many people confuse the two. Those who communicate assertively stand up for their own rights and present themselves and their ideas with forthrightness and strength. Those who communicate aggressively also do this; however, an aggressive communicator also demands that others yield to his rights. A person communicating assertively makes requests. A person communicating aggressively makes demands. A person communicating assertively insists that his rights be respected. A person communicating aggressively does the same while ignoring the rights of others.

Research indicates that both assertiveness and aggressiveness have a strong negative correlation with communication apprehension. That is, the more apprehensive a person is about communication, the less likely he is to behave in either an assertive or an aggressive manner. This fact has both good and bad implications for the effectiveness of the high communication apprehensives' communication. Since aggressive communication is likely to alienate other people, at least the highly apprehensive person is unlikely to face this outcome. On the other hand, unassertive people tend to be taken advantage of or are ignored by others, no matter how right they may be. In addition, they tend to be looked upon as ineffectual people by others in their environment.

Engaging in assertive communication behavior in most cases prompts other people in an interaction to communicate more. Highly apprehensive people, of course, tend to avoid communication, particularly communication that involves interpersonal conflict, since this is what makes them most uncomfortable. Thus, quiet persons often will simply yield their rights (be unassertive) rather than defend them (be assertive) in order to avoid more communication. Consequently, high communication apprehensives or quiet people frequently are not seen as effective communicators as they would like to be.

Responsiveness

Responsiveness is the capacity to be sensitive to the communication of others, to be seen as a good listener, to make others comfortable in communicating, and to recognize the needs and desires of others. In some research, this aspect of communication is stereotyped as "femininity." This does not mean that only females are responsive, but the communication behaviors most closely associated with responsiveness are similar to the traditional U.S. stereotype of appropriate communication behaviors for females.

When you examine the measure in Appendix O, note that such qualities as "sympathetic," "compassionate," "gentle," and "friendly" are associated with the responsiveness construct. Although such terms do describe the stereotypical female image in U.S. society, they more importantly describe a person who is open to the communication of others as well as being empathic.

It is important to distinguish between responsiveness and submissiveness, since many people confuse the two. Submissiveness is the yielding of one's legitimate rights to another without necessarily receiving anything in return. Responsiveness is recognizing the needs and rights of another without yielding one's own rights. The responsive individual communicates understanding and acknowledgment of the feelings of the other person. The submissive individual might also do this but then go on to yield to the requests of the other person even when it requires that he or she go against her or his own feelings, rights, or needs.

Considerable research indicates that communication apprehension is correlated with both responsiveness and submissiveness; however, the directions of the correlations are different. Communication apprehension is positively correlated with submissiveness but negatively correlated with responsiveness. The highly communicative apprehensive individual (the quiet person) is likely to submit to the desires of another because the failure to do so might prompt more communication attempts from the other person, at best, and communication involving conflict, at worst. In order to avoid these outcomes, the highly communication apprehensive individual (the quiet person) simply submits.

Rawpixel/Shutterstock.com

The amount of physical distance between people is one of the strongest indicators of immediacy.

In contrast, the highly communication apprehensive individual (the quiet person) is much less likely to communicate in a responsive manner. Most of the behaviors that indicate responsiveness are invitations to additional communication, which the person wants to avoid. The primary way in which we communicate responsiveness to others is through immediacy (or verbal closeness) with them, and research indicates there is a substantial negative correlation between communication apprehension and immediacy in communication. (We discuss immediacy in a later section.) The higher the level of communication apprehension, the less immediacy expressed in the communication of the individual. Consequently, highly communication apprehensive individuals frequently are ineffective communicators in the area of responsiveness. Unfortunately, people who are not immediate and responsive tend to be perceived negatively by others. They typically are seen as cold and unfriendly, even uncaring; consequently, they might not seem attractive as potential friends and colleagues.

Versatility

The final important characteristic of the effective communicator is versatility. Versatility is the capacity to be appropriately assertive and appropriately responsive, depending on the situation. People who are versatile in their communication behaviors can be described as accommodating, adaptable, informal, and willing to adjust to others. People not exhibiting versatility in their communication can be described as rigid, inflexible, unyielding, and uncompromising.

Some situations call for high assertiveness or high responsiveness, for low assertiveness or low responsiveness. Some situations call for both high assertiveness and responsiveness, but very few call for low levels of both. Individuals who are versatile in their communication behaviors are able to adapt to these disparate demands of situations. Individuals who tend to have habitual communication behavior patterns are insensitive to the varying demands of situations.

Communicating effectively with different people on different topics and at different times requires flexible communication behaviors. Consider, for example, the situation in which you might be communicating with a highly aggressive individual. Should you be highly assertive in response or highly responsive? The former choice might lead to confrontation and conflict, the latter to submission. Neither would normally be seen as the "best" way to communicate. The most effective communicator would be assertive when necessary to defend his own rights but remain responsive to the other's communication without submitting to unreasonable requests or demands. An outside observer would see the competent individual behaving differently at different points in the interaction.

In contrast with the versatile communicator in the example above, people lacking versatility in their communication behavior tend to be assertive or nonassertive and responsive or nonresponsive nearly all the time. Such people might be stereotyped by their characteristic communication behaviors. The person who is characteristically highly assertive but nonresponsive has been labeled "masculine," in keeping with the male stereotype in the U.S. culture. The opposite stereotype, highly responsive but nonassertive, has been labeled "feminine," again in keeping with the female stereotype in the United States.

The person who is both highly assertive and highly responsive has been labeled "androgynous." Although this person is just as strongly stereotyped as the others, in the U.S. culture this type of characteristic communication pattern tends to be much more effective in most cases. This probably is a result of the two sets of behaviors (assertive and responsive) balancing each other out to prevent excesses that might otherwise result from either. High assertiveness is prevented from becoming aggressiveness by the presence of high responsiveness. Similarly, high responsiveness is prevented from becoming submissiveness by the presence of high assertiveness. Although this person might not truly be versatile, it is likely he will be perceived as such by others.

At the other end of the continuum, is the individual who is both nonassertive and nonresponsive. This individual also lacks versatility, and, unlike the androgynous individual, it is highly unlikely others will see this person as versatile. Research has found a high proportion of these individuals to be high communication apprehensives (Lashbrook, Knutson, Parsley, & Wenburg, 1976) or people who have a low willingness to communicate with others. These individuals are the ones least likely to be effective communicators. The only way these individuals can become more effective communicators is to reduce their communication apprehension and anxiety.

Immediacy

Immediacy is the degree of perceived physical or psychological closeness between two people. The concept is best understood in terms of the "immediacy principle" as outlined by Mehrabian (1971), who introduced this concept. This principle is as follows, "People are drawn toward persons and things they like, evaluate highly, and prefer; and they avoid or move away from things they dislike, evaluate negatively, or do not prefer" (p. 1).

In connection with our discussion above, responsive communication behaviors are those that are immediate, and nonresponsive communication behaviors are those that are nonimmediate. Responsiveness on the part of another, then, makes us feel that they, like us, evaluate us highly, and prefer to interact with us. In contrast, nonresponsiveness on the part of another makes us feel they dislike us, evaluate us negatively, and prefer not to interact with us (Richmond et al., 1991).

Immediacy behaviors generate these perceptions and are important in two ways: They are the primary means of expressing approval of another, and they provide an invitation to another to continue communication. In order to understand immediacy and its relationship to communication apprehension, avoidance, and effectiveness, it is important to look at specific behaviors that express varying degrees of immediacy.

Verbal Immediacy

What people say causes us to feel either closer to or more distant from them. Increased immediacy is produced by verbal messages indicating openness to the other, friendship for the other, or empathy with the other. Such simple things as the use of the pronoun "we" rather than "you," or "you and I," or "us" can increase feelings of immediacy.

One of the most important ways of increasing immediacy in a relationship is by sending verbal messages that encourage the other person to communicate. Such comments as "I see/what you mean;" "Tell me more;" "That is a good point;" and "I think so, too" will create increased immediacy. Contrast these comments with the following: "Oh, shut up;" "That is stupid;" "I thought of that years ago;" and "Frankly, I don't care what you think." If you were to hear any of the latter comments, would you want to communicate more? How close would you feel to the person who made such a comment?

Clearly, the most direct way to modify feelings of immediacy is through verbal messages. It is important to note, however, that many nonverbal messages can accomplish the same end, although they often are much less direct. Although immediacy is communicated both verbally and nonverbally, the nonverbal component appears to be far more important in most cases; while the nonverbal might exist independent of any verbal message, they are almost always accompanied by a variety of nonverbal messages (Richmond et al., 1991). Furthermore, if a verbal message indicates immediacy while nonverbal messages are contradictory, receivers tend to disregard the verbal message.

Nonverbal Immediacy

The following discussions outline some of the important nonverbal message systems. Each is related to nonverbal immediacy.

Space The amount of physical distance between people is one of the strongest indicators of immediacy. How do you feel when you try to stand or sit close to someone and that person keeps moving away? Regardless of the reason for moving, you probably interpret the behavior as rejection. In order to be perceived as immediate, a person needs to reduce the physical distance between himself and the other person. Extremely close physical proximity, of course, is reserved for intimate communication. To try to establish such extreme closeness in a nonintimate relationship is likely to be perceived negatively by the other person.

Touch Touch is the ultimate method used to reduce physical distance. As such it is the most immediate nonverbal behavior. Many people consider touch to be the most potent form of communication. As a result, when it is appropriate, it strongly communicates immediacy. When it is inappropriate, however, it is likely to be interpreted negatively. Contrast, for example, a pat on a friend's back for a job well done with a pat on the backside of a stranger in an elevator. Both are touch. One is an appropriate immediacy behavior; the other might prompt a call for the police.

Eye Behavior Eye contact reduces perceived physical distance. When people look at us when we are talking, we feel closer to them. If their eyes are wandering around the room, we quickly realize they do not care about what we are saying and possibly not even about us. People sitting eight feet apart with constant eye contact might feel closer to one another than people sitting three feet apart with no eye contact. As with space and touch, too much of a good thing causes problems. Constant eye contact, particularly at close distances, might be interpreted as staring and make the recipient of the eye contact very uncomfortable.

Facial Expression In addition to our eyes, the rest of our face can also communicate immediacy. In particular, a smile is seen as an immediate nonverbal message. A frown, of course, is seen as nonimmediate. We also communicate attention, or lack of same, by our facial expression and eye behavior. This is not just a matter of eye contact, but also the expression around the eyes and mouths. An attentive expression is a strong immediacy behavior.

Gestures and Bodily Movements The position of your body when communicating with another, your posture, the type and amount of gestures you employ all involve immediacy messages. The person who seems relaxed, has an open body position, leans forward when communicating, and gestures in a positive manner is likely to be perceived as immediate. Nonimmediate behaviors include such things as a closed body position (like arms folded across each other), very little gesturing, and a tense posture. Of course, gestures and bodily movements can be overdone, like most other immediacy behaviors. When they are we sometimes refer to the person as "coming on like gangbusters." Such behaviors can become too much and cease to be immediate.

Voice One of the subtlest ways we communicate immediacy is through our voices. A high degree of voice variety is immediate, while a monotone voice is one of the most nonimmediate communication behaviors. In a recent study, we found that the nonverbal behavior that most distinguished students' perceptions between good and poor teachers was vocal variety. This is also strongly correlated with the amount students reported learning in classes. If people have little vocal animation when they talk with us, they communicate that they do not care about us and/or what they are talking about. We may in turn conclude that we have little reason to care about what they are saying.

Scent It is clear from the research that odor can evoke emotional and even physical responses from people and animals. Humans have learned to manipulate scent to produce certain reactions. Men and women wear

An attentive expression is a strong nonverbal immediacy behavior.

scents they think will attract one another. Researchers generally agree that overpowering scents, offensive scents, and unfamiliar scents tend to make people nonimmediate with others or the environment. We are not as likely to seek immediacy with a person who has offensive body odor or overpowering cologne—we prefer familiar, subtle scents.

Time An immediacy behavior often overlooked is the amount of time we spend with someone. For the most part, the more time we spend with another individual, the more immediate we are with her or him. Contrast, for example, the teacher who is willing to take an extra half-hour in her or his office to explain something to you with the teacher who tells you to look it up in your textbook. You are probably going to see the former teacher as much more immediate.

Immediacy and Communication Apprehension

The relationships between immediacy behaviors and communication apprehension and avoidance are strong. Since people who are apprehensive about communicating generally wish to avoid communicating, and immediacy behaviors are an invitation to continued communication, such people tend to be much less immediate than others. By being nonimmediate with others in the environment, highly apprehensive individuals cause the others to have a reduced desire to communicate with them. Thus, the apprehensive individual is involved in less total communication because they choose not to initiate communication with others and because the others choose not to initiate communication with them.

The reduced immediacy behaviors of the quiet person also lead them to be less effective communicators when they do communicate. This can be explained in part by the "principle of reciprocity." In communication situations, there is a strong tendency for people to imitate the behavior of others with whom they do communicate. In other words, communication patterns tend to be reciprocal: I do what you do and you do what I do. If one person smiles or exhibits some other immediate behavior, it is increasingly likely the other person will engage in similar behavior. It is often said the best way to make a friend is to be a friend. This is the reciprocity principle in action. This tends to interfere with the attempts of the apprehensive individuals to communicate effectively with other people at such times as they do try to do so.

Quite simply, then, high communication apprehension and a low willingness to communicate tend to lead to ineffective communication. The only solution to this problem is to reduce the apprehension and anxiety and become more willing to communicate with others. It is easier to suggest than to do. Hence, Chapter 7 is directed toward methods that have been found helpful in accomplishing the above objective.

DISCUSSION QUESTIONS

1. Although communication scholars are far from being in agreement as to what actually constitutes "communication competence," they are in agreement that to be competent is to be an effective communicator. What is meant by the above statement? Can you give further explanations for what constitutes communication competence?
2. Why is it an impossible task "to determine precisely what will make a communicator effective in every possible situation?"?
3. According to the text, what is the most common acceptable definition of communication competence?
4. What are the three major elements that appear to have the most impact on the development of effective communication? How does each of these have an impact on effective communication skills?
5. According to the text, self-perceived communication competence has been found to correlate positively with which variables? To correlate negatively with which variables?
6. Who generated the early research in the social style area? What is the definition of *social style* and the three important elements?
7. How are social style and its three components related to communication competence?
8. What is immediacy? What is the difference between nonverbal immediacy and verbal immediacy?
9. What are some important nonverbal messages associated with nonverbal immediacy? How is immediacy related to communication competence?
10. How does the "principle of reciprocity" work for and against individuals?

ACTIVITIES

1. Complete the Self-Perceived Communication Competence (SPCC, Appendix J) scale. Examine the four basic communication contexts and three types of receivers and determine where you need to gain competence. Examine your total SPCC score and devise solutions to improve your communication competence.
2. Compare your scores on the SPCC (Appendix J) with other measures such as the WTC (Appendix C), PRCA-24 (Appendix F), and Introversion Scale (Appendix A). See if you can determine the area(s) where you feel insecure about when communicating and try to generate ideas on how to improve your communication in those areas.

3. Complete the Sociocommunicative Orientation Scale (Appendix O) and determine if you need to improve your assertiveness, responsiveness, or versatility skills. For example: (1) decide if you are aggressive as opposed to assertive, then determine how you might approach situations assertively, not aggressively; (2) decide if you are submissive as opposed to assertive, then determine how you might approach situations assertively, not submissively; (3) decide if you are not responsive, then determine how you can become more responsive to the needs of others; and (4) decide if you are rigid in your communication, then determine how you can become more versatile. Finally, what communication traits decrease your likelihood of being a more versatile communicator?

4. Generate ways in which you could use nonverbal immediacy and verbal immediacy to improve your communication effectiveness. Think about how to employ the immediacy behaviors to show approval of others and to encourage others to communicate with you.

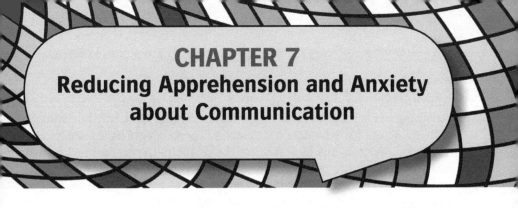

CHAPTER 7
Reducing Apprehension and Anxiety about Communication

In the preceding chapters of this text, we discussed the nature of human communication and the impact it has on our lives and relationships when we avoid it, are scared by it, or are apprehensive and unwilling to communicate effectively. It is clear that for many people communication apprehension is the single most important factor contributing to a lack of effective communication. In this chapter, we direct our attention to five methods that have been developed to help people reduce apprehension and anxiety about communication: (1) systematic desensitization, (2) cognitive restructuring, (3) skills training, (4) visualization, and (5) psychopharmacology.

In order to understand the differences in these methods, it's necessary to become familiar with the divergent theories concerned with why people are apprehensive. Each of the three methods developed as a result of a different view of the cause of the problem.

Theories of Causes

The basic theories about why people experience fear or anxiety about communication are placed into four categories: (1) excessive activation, (2) inappropriate cognitive processing, (3) inadequate communication skills, and (4) biological determinism.

Excessive Activation

If you can recall the first time you ever had to speak, sing, play a ball game, or otherwise perform before a group of people, you will probably remember your heart beating rapidly, your palms getting wet with sweat, and possibly remember a slight feeling of queasiness in your stomach and a headache or neck ache. All of these physiological reactions are symptoms of your body preparing for the upcoming performance. Athletes often refer to this as "getting psyched up" before a game. This increase in the physiological activation in your body is altogether normal. In fact, such an increase in activation often is essential to a quality performance.

Increased activation is one thing, however, and excessive activation is quite another. Excessive activation occurs when the normal increase in activation in anticipation of a performance continues to a point beyond an individual's ability to control it. In extreme cases, people have been known to regurgitate their meals, to faint, and to urinate. In rare instances, such excessive activation can even prompt a heart attack. Much more commonly, however, excessive activation brings on trembling arms, hands, and legs; shortness of breath; dry mouth; swallowing difficulty; tense muscles; and temporary memory loss.

From the first theoretical viewpoint, these bodily disturbances are what make up apprehension—a physiological overreaction to an upcoming performance. This theory might be thought of as a purely behavioral interpretation of the problem. It gives no mental explanation, simply posits that what one thinks is of no importance, but what one's body is doing is critical.

Since physiological arousal is the cause of the problem, the obvious solution is to reduce that arousal, and many methods to do so have been found to be temporarily effective. These include hypnotism, meditation, the use of biofeedback, and ingestion of certain medications; however, learning deep muscular relaxation techniques has the most long-term positive impact. Such relaxation is the main component of treating communication apprehension (as well as other phobic anxieties). This method is known as "systematic desensitization." If one is to operate on the basis of the excessive activation theory, this method is appropriate.

Inappropriate Cognitive Processing

Research indicates that many people who are highly aroused physiologically do not report being apprehensive about the upcoming communication situation (or performance), while others with similar high arousal report extreme apprehension. In addition, some people with much lower levels of arousal report high levels of apprehension while others similarly aroused do not.

This leads many people to believe the problem is caused not by one's body, but by one's mind. This view sees people who report experiencing high apprehension in a communication situation as having reactions no different from other people, except that they think they are different. In short, this view sees the person who reports experiencing high apprehension as simply processing the available information inappropriately. One person perceives physiological activation as evidence he is excited, while another person perceives it as evidence he is terrified. The problem, therefore, is in the cognitive processing of the individual.

This theoretical view is a cognitive rather than a behavioral one. Since the problem is seen as being all in one's mind, the solution of the problem is to change the person's mind. A method known as "cognitive restructuring," based on this view, was developed to overcome communication apprehension in addition to other phobic anxieties.

At first examination, it might appear that the excessive activation and inappropriate cognitive processing theories are contradictory; if one is correct, the other must be incorrect. Although some people who are strongly committed to one or the other of the theories have argued this position, research suggests both are at least partially correct.

An important study by Behnke and Beatty (1981) sheds the most light on this area. The researchers asked subjects who had just given a public speech to indicate how much anxiety they felt during the speech. The researchers also measured the speakers' levels of physiological activation during the speech (their heart rates) and, as a measure of how they cognitively process information about communication, obtained responses from the subjects on the Personal Report of Communication Apprehension (PRCA).

Research results indicate that heart rates while speaking are not correlated with PRCA scores, suggesting that physiological activation and cognitive processing may not be meaningfully related. Both heart rate and PRCA scores, however, are highly related to the amount of anxiety the subjects reported experiencing while speaking. In fact, the two variables together account for almost 80% of the variability in self-reported anxiety while speaking.

On the basis of this study, it appears these two theories are not in conflict with each other. Rather, it appears both are correct, but apply differently to different people. Some people experience anxiety while communicating because their bodies are excessively activated. Others experience anxiety because they are cognitively predispositioned to interpret whatever activation is present, even if it is low, as indicating they are anxious.

We know from additional research that the cognitive processing a person does can have an impact on physical health, attitudes, outlook, and even mental health. In fact, there is a relationship between people's cognitive processing and how well they cope with tense or conflict-like situations. Some people simply cope better than others. Some people can cognitively process information to their advantage, others cannot. Persons who are highly aroused mentally in a negative way need to cognitively restructure the way they think about situations.

Inadequate Communication Skills

Probably the oldest and most persistent view of why people are apprehensive about communication is that they are fearful and anxious because they do not know how to communicate effectively. There are certainly many people who are deficient in communication skills, particularly the kinds of cognitive communication skills we discussed in Chapter 6. There are also some who are deficient in behavioral skills. If one does not know how to do something, but is forced to do it anyway, to be fearful or anxious is a normal reaction. For example, if you do not know how to drive a car, but must do so in an emergency, if you are not afraid you are not normal. The obvious method to help a person overcome communication apprehension—if it stems from a lack of communication skills—is to provide training to improve the skills. That indeed is the method advocated by people who subscribe to this theory. The major problem with this approach, however, is that research has not provided much evidence to support it. In fact, studies that involved direct observation of the communication behaviors of high and low apprehensives mostly failed to find any differences in the actual communication skills of the two groups. The subjects in the two groups, however, consistently believed their skill levels were different. The highly apprehensive subjects thought their skills deficient while the subjects with lower apprehension did not. Yet on the basis of direct observation by the researcher, some subjects in both groups were found to have high skills, and some to have low skills.

Results of this type of research suggest deficient skills alone might be insufficient to cause apprehension. Thus, it might be more of how one thinks about her or his skills than the actual skill level that is important. This, of course, relates back to the inappropriate cognitive processing explanation. This could explain why the skills-training approach that seems to be most effective in helping people is the method known as "rhetoritherapy," developed by Phillips (1977). This method, unlike other skills approaches, includes a strong component of cognitive restructuring in addition to training involving specific skills.

Biological Determinism

Fear is a tricky primal instinct. We live in a world of scary creatures and situations. From walking in the woods and stumbling upon a rattlesnake, bear, or mountain lion to riding in an elevator that suddenly drops a few floors, many things can induce fear in humans. Historically, we (from an evolutionary perspective) developed our sense of fear as a method to protect ourselves.

In 1970, Martin Seligman proposed what has become known as the *preparedness principle*. In short, the preparedness principle states that individuals are hard-wired to respond to specific stimuli as a result of genetics. For example, many people do not need to have come in contact with a rattlesnake or be told that a rattlesnake is dangerous to have an actual fear of rattlesnakes. As such, Seligman postulated that some stimuli trigger genetically fear-based associations with objects or situations because evolutionarily their ancestors learned that some objects and situations are dangerous and fear-invoking and should be avoided. In essence, fear response is in part an aspect of Darwin's natural selection—our ancestors learned to avoid objects and situations that would have otherwise gotten them killed and then passed on their genes to future generations with those fears encoded in their DNA. Seligman did not believe that all fears were arrived at in this manner, but a great many of our deeply rooted fears are.

In 1971, Seligman tested his hypothesis to great success. Overall, Seligman found that:

> the fears of individuals diagnosed with phobias reflect evolutionarily prepared learning to fear events and situations that have provided survival threats in an evolutionary rather than in a contemporary perspective. Thus, there are phobias for snakes and other threatening animals, thunder and lightning, heights, closed as well as wide-open places, and *social evaluations, e.g., when addressing an audience,* but not for contemporary threats to health and wellbeing, such as bikes, motorcycles, broken electrical equipment, or handguns [emphasis added].
>
> (Öhman, 2009, p. 543)

Seligman argues that those fears that have been around for centuries may be ones genetically hardwired into us, which is why people react negatively to certain perceived threats even if they have had no contact with that threat prior to the exposure. Although Seligman's theory of why we have developed certain fears is not without controversy within the academic community, it does provide one explanation for why people react to certain fears without exposure to specific objects or situations.

In the field of communication, new research has recently provided another biologically-based understanding for communication apprehension. In an article by Beatty, Heisel, Lewis, Pence, Reinhart, and Tian (2011), the researchers examined the possibility of a relationship between individuals with high levels of communication apprehension and resting alpha range asymmetry in the anterior cortex (AC). Using data collected through an electroencephalograph (EEG), the researchers were able to determine that there is a moderate relationship between resting AC levels and CA. The researchers ultimately conclude, "Our findings suggest a sizable chunk of the variance in trait-like CA resides in an inborn, stable pattern of electrical functioning in the AC while communicators are at rest. Whether this feature of neurobiology and the aspect of trait-like CA implemented by it are susceptible to behavior modification is an empirical matter" (p. 454). For more on the increasing research examining the biological underpinnings of human communication, we would recommend reading Beatty, McCroskey, and Floyd's (2009) book.

Treatment Approaches

A number of books and hundreds of popular press articles have appeared over the past few years professing to help people overcome shyness, reticence, or communication apprehension. All provide so-called self-help methods that allegedly allow readers to solve their problems. All evidence indicates that such writings do not work. A careful examination of the research literature fails to produce a single study providing reliable data to the contrary. Real help must come from a formal treatment program under the guidance of a trained professional.

When we think of "treatment," we tend to think of medical treatment. Most medical treatment is based on a physician diagnosing a patient and then prescribing a drug or performing an operation to overcome the problem. Treatment of communication apprehension is not analogous to medical treatment. Rather, all treatments involve the person in charge of the treatment working with a client in a joint effort to overcome the problem. In this sense, treatment for communication apprehension more closely resembles preventive medicine than medical treatment.

To improve a patient's health, for example, a physician might outline a diet. However, it is up to the patient to follow the diet. Similarly, in the treatment of communication apprehension the person guiding the treatment might outline the steps an individual should follow to obtain improvement, but it is up to the individual to do what is necessary to obtain the desired benefits. In both cases (preventive medicine and treatment for communication apprehension), the individual must want to obtain the benefits and be committed to following the advice of the professional for any improvement to occur. In the absence of such commitment, no improvement is likely. As stated earlier, the five most commonly employed methods for treating communication apprehension are (1) systematic desensitization, (2) cognitive restructuring, (3) skills training, (4) visualization, and (5) psychopharmacology.

Systematic Desensitization

Systematic desensitization (SD) is a behavior therapy originally developed by Wolpe (1958). The method was used in a major study conducted by Paul (1966) involving apprehension about public speaking and was introduced as a method of treating more broadly based communication apprehension by McCroskey, Ralph, and Barrick (1970) and again by McCroskey (1972). It is now the most widely used method in the communication field (Hoffman & Sprague, 1982). There are two primary components in the systematic desensitization method:

1. Teaching the subjects the procedures for deep muscular relaxation.
2. Having the subjects visualize participating in a series of communication situations while in a state of deep relaxation.

The series is ordered from the least anxiety-provoking situation (talking to your best friend) to the most anxiety-provoking situation (you are to appear on a television show and can't find your notes or you have been asked to speak, without any time to prepare, to a large group about your ideas on peace). The treatment might be administered either on an individual basis or in a small group, normally 5 to 7 people. A typical program includes 5 to 7 one-hour sessions spread over several days or several weeks.

First Session, Step 1 The helper explains the program to the participants, usually stressing that the treatment does not involve the subject having to engage in any type of communication activity. Rather, it is explained, the subject will (1) learn how to achieve deep muscular relaxation, and (2) will be trained to maintain relaxation while visualizing participating in increasingly more stressful communication experiences. If the participants have any questions, the helper answers them, then the actual treatment begins.

Step 2 Participants are seated in comfortable chairs and told to lean back and relax. The communication system between the subjects and the helper is then explained. The participants are told that anytime they feel tension, once the relaxation instructions have been provided, they are to signal the helper simply by raising the index finger of their right hand. This is also noted as the method of responding to any questions that the helper might ask later in the session.

Step 3 Once the helper is certain the participants understand the procedure for communicating tension, the helper turns on a prerecorded tape that includes instructions for deep muscular relaxation. This tape instructs the participants to tense and relax each of the major muscle groups in the body. The total time for this instructional process is about 25 minutes. (An example of the relaxation exercises is provided below.)

Step 4 When the instructions for relaxation have been completed, the helper turns off the recorder and checks to make certain all of the participants are awake. This is necessary because in a state of deep relaxation people tend to fall asleep. When the helper is confident all of the participants are awake and deeply relaxed, the helper reminds them that if at any time they feel tension they should raise their index finger. Then the helper asks the participants to visualize themselves in the least-threatening communication situation, such as, "You are talking to your best friend." (An example of nonthreatening to threatening communication situations is provided on pages 135 and 136.) The helper then remains silent for a period of approximately 15 seconds while watching for finger indications of tension. If any participant signals tension, the helper asks all participants to put the situation out of their minds and then provides a few moments of relaxation instructions similar to those on the prerecorded tape. If no participant indicates tension for 15 seconds, the helper directs all participants to put the situation out of their minds and provides a few moments of relaxation instructions before visualizing the situation again.

If any participant signals tension, the process of visualization is continuously repeated, until no participant does so for 15 seconds. Then, after a few moments of relaxation instructions, the visualization is repeated with the helper waiting 30 seconds before terminating the visualization unless a participant signals that he or she is experiencing tension. If there is such a signal, the same procedure used with the 15-second interval is employed. The process is repeated until all participants have been able to visualize the situation for 15 to 30 seconds sequentially without experiencing tension.

Speaker speaking in an empty auditorium

Hero Images/Getty Images

Step 5 At this point the helper moves on to the second communication situation and repeats exactly the procedure used with the first communication situation. This process is continued until all of the communication situations have been successfully visualized without tension by all participants in the group or until the time to end the session is near. If the number of situations to which the participants are to be exposed is typical (16 to 18), the entire list will not be completed in the first session, nor likely even in the first four or five sessions.

Step 6 To complete a given session, the helper will have the participants visualize a situation they have already successfully visualized without tension for approximately 60 seconds. This will help ensure that the participants are still deeply relaxed as the session ends. At this point the helper typically asks the participants to open their eyes and gradually become reacquainted with their surroundings. After the participants have become more alert, the helper suggests they practice the relaxation exercises daily in between sessions and to use them to become relaxed if they confront stressful communication situations during the intervening time period.

Subsequent Sessions The same procedures are followed as in the first session with only minor variations. In later sessions, it might not be necessary to play the entire tape of relaxation instructions. This is particularly true if the participants have been given copies of the tape in order to practice between sessions. Also in later sessions, the helper might begin with somewhat more stressful communication situations than the original one, but avoids starting with any situation that prompted tension in the preceding session. After two or three sessions, helpers ask the participants to relate their outside experiences in attempting to use the learned techniques in real communication situations. This helps to reinforce that participants should be making such attempts.

Conclusions about Systematic Desensitization Treatment Ideally, sessions should continue until all participants are able to visualize all of the communication situations without experiencing tension. If this is accomplished before the scheduled number of sessions has been held (normally 5 to 7), the program can be terminated early. If this has not been accomplished when the last scheduled session is completed, additional sessions should be added. If one individual in a group seems to be reacting with significantly more tension than the other members, it might be necessary to remove that person from later sessions in order for the remaining group members to complete the entire program. It is relatively rare that such a person is found in a group since the treatment is so highly effective; however, there are people who are not helped by the method and who continue to respond with high tension during the treatment sessions. For this small percentage, one of the other methods described should be substituted.

Systematic desensitization is an extremely effective method for helping people overcome communication apprehension. Research indicates approximately 90% of the people who receive this treatment reduce their levels of communication apprehension. Of those who enter the treatment as high communication apprehensives, 80% are no longer high apprehensives after treatment. As we noted earlier, systematic desensitization is the most appropriate method of treating communication apprehension if one presumes the problem stems from excessive physiological activation. McCroskey, Ralph, and Barrick (1968) tested to determine the effects of this method on such activation. They found that measured heart-rate activation in participants reporting anxiety greatly increased as they were exposed to a formal communication situation prior to treatment. After treatment, however, these same participants were able to control their activation so that no similar increase occurred. The effectiveness of systematic desensitization is not restricted to simply increasing control of activation. A number of studies (McCroskey, 1972) have found cognitive effects in terms of substantially reduced scores on the Personal Report of Communication Apprehension. In addition, Goss, Thompson, and Olds (1978) reported meaningful improvements in communication behavior as well. Although the exact reason why systematic desensitization works remains a subject of scholarly dispute; that it works and works well is clearly established.

Examples of Muscle Relaxation

Based on the work of Wolpe, SD is a treatment program that includes training in deep muscular relaxation, a hierarchy of anxiety-eliciting stimuli, and the pairing, through imagery, of the anxiety-producing stimuli on the hierarchy with relaxation. For the muscle groups listed below, you usually hold or tense the muscle for several seconds, then relax and mentally note how good the relaxation feels. Using Jacobson's (1938) progressive muscle relaxation training the following muscles are tensed then relaxed:

1. Hands (clench and unclench right hand, then left hand).
2. Biceps and triceps (bend right hand upward at wrist, pointing fingers toward ceiling, relax, then left hand; bring both hands up toward shoulders, flex biceps, then relax, repeat).
3. Shoulders (shrug shoulders, hold, relax).
4. Neck (push head against chair, relax; lean forward, relax).
5. Mouth (press lips tightly together, then relax).
6. Tongue (extend, hold, retract).

7. Tongue (press mouth roof, relax; press mouth floor, relax).
8. Eyes and forehead (close eyes tightly, relax; wrinkle forehead, relax).
9. Breathing (inhale, hold, exhale).
10. Back (arch back, hold, relax).
11. Midsection (tense muscles including buttocks, hold, relax).
12. Thighs (tense muscles, hold, relax).
13. Stomach (suck in stomach, hold, relax).
14. Calves and feet (stretch out both legs, hold, relax).
15. Toes (point toes toward ceiling, hold, relax; point toes downward, hold, relax).

Again, much repetition might take place in each muscle group to become totally relaxed. Usually, each group is tensed and relaxed at least two times before moving on to the next muscle group. A common range is 5–10 seconds for tensing a muscle and 10–15 seconds for relaxation.

Samples of Nonthreatening to Threatening Communication Situations

(Note: The entire hierarchy can be built around a single fear or single situation.)

1. You are talking to your best friend on the phone.
2. You are talking to your best friend in person.
3. You are being introduced to a new acquaintance by your best friend.
4. You are introducing yourself to a new acquaintance.
5. You are talking to an operator about placing a long-distance phone call.
6. You are talking to a clerk in a department store.
7. You have to talk to a small group of people, all of whom you know well.
8. You are talking to a supervisor or someone who is in a supervisory role, such as a teacher, about a problem at work/school.
9. You are at a social gathering where you don't know anyone, but are expected to meet and talk to others.
10. You are going to ask someone to go to a movie with you.
11. You are going to ask someone to go to a party with you.
12. You have to talk to a law-enforcement officer about a ticket.
13. You are going on a job interview.
14. You have been asked to give a presentation in front of a large group of people.

15. You are getting ready to give a public speech but realize you left your notes at home.
16. You are to appear on a panel television show with others and talk about a topic you know well.
17. You are to appear on a television show and debate another person.
18. You are ready to appear on a television show and give a speech, but you lost your notes.

Cognitive Restructuring

The method of cognitive restructuring (Meichenbaum, 1976) evolved from an earlier method known as "rational-emotive therapy" (Ellis, 1962). Both are based on the idea that people have irrational thoughts about themselves and their behaviors and that these thoughts increase the anxiety a person is likely to have about situations such as communicating with others. In rational-emotive therapy, the person receiving treatment is encouraged to identify irrational beliefs they have about communication, and then these beliefs are attacked logically in an attempt to demonstrate to the individual that the person should change her or his way of thinking. The assumption is that if the irrational thoughts are eliminated, the apprehension will be reduced. Several research studies indicate that this approach has some positive effect.

The cognitive restructuring approach goes one step further. In addition to identifying the illogical beliefs held by the individual, the helper assists the individual in formulating new, more appropriate beliefs. This method recognizes that simple elimination of illogical beliefs might not be enough and that the replacement of displaced beliefs by more appropriate beliefs is an important positive step.

Like systematic desensitization, cognitive restructuring typically is administered in five or six one-hour sessions spread over several days or weeks. Treatment might be administered to people on an individual basis or in small groups, typically four to eight people. As outlined by Fremouw (1984), the treatment involves four steps:

1. Introduction of the person being treated to the method;
2. Identification of negative self-statements (illogical beliefs);
3. Learning coping statements (beliefs to replace the illogical ones);
4. Practice.

First Session During the first session, the helper gives the participants in the treatment program a thorough rationale and purpose for the program. He explains that communication apprehension is a learned reaction that most people can change in a few hours. It is explained that people mentally talk to themselves and that the self-statements they make might be completely irrational and harmful. Finally, it is explained that by learning positive coping statements to substitute for the harmful ones, the participants can reduce their apprehension.

Following this introduction, the participants are encouraged to identify specific negative self-statements or thoughts that increase apprehension. The helper provides a large number of examples to illustrate the kind of statement under consideration; for instance, "I'll die if I have to give a speech;" "This interview is the most important thing in my life;" "No one will like me if I don't do well;" and "I don't know how to ask for a date." After the participants understand what negative self-statements are, they are each asked to identify and write down three or four that they commonly make to themselves. These are then discussed by the helper in terms of how they might affect a person's feeling about communication as well as their behavior. Logical errors ("If everyone does not agree with me, I have failed") and self-fulfilling prophecies ("I will do a miserable job") are pointed out also. At the conclusion of the first session, participants are asked to continue to be aware of the negative self-statements they make to themselves regarding communication. They are encouraged to write down these statements and bring them to the second session.

Second Session This session begins with a discussion of the negative self-statements that the participants bring in, for examples of statements they have used since the previous session. This is handled in much the same way as were the negative self-statements in the first session. When this is completed, the helper works with the participants to generate positive self-statements (coping statements), which can be substituted for the negative ones. Different groups of statements are generated for use before, during, and after the communication event. Examples of such statements might be: "Most of these people really want to hear my ideas;" "This really is quite easy;" and "I did a good job." At the conclusion of this session, the participants are encouraged to attempt to substitute the positive self-statements for the negative ones when they communicate with others before the next session.

Subsequent Sessions The remaining sessions are devoted to guided practice in using the coping statements. Participants are placed in groups (unless they are already in a group for treatment) and asked to discuss topics of an increasingly controversial nature. The participants are also asked to keep a diary identifying stressful communication situations they have experienced both within the treatment sessions and between sessions, describing the coping statements they used in those situations. When all of the participants report they have used coping statements in stressful communication situations, the practice sessions are terminated, and the treatment program is complete.

Conclusions about Cognitive Restructuring Research involving cognitive restructuring indicates it is effective in accomplishing its specific objective-reducing self-reported apprehension about communication. Its effectiveness seems to be roughly equal to that of systematic desensitization in this regard. There is evidence cognitive restructuring also reduces observable manifestations of anxiety in communication encounters.

Some treatment programs have been developed that include both the cognitive restructuring and the systematic desensitization methods. Research indicates that the two together are more effective than either is alone, but as yet there is insufficient data to be certain this is the case. Current research, however, suggests that systematic desensitization should first be administered, then cognitive restructuring.

More recently, some research has been attempting to help people bridge the gap between old versions of cognitive restructuring, which was all conducted inside someone's head, and helping people visualize the public speaking context in a controlled environment through the use of virtual reality. Virtual reality training (VRT) enables users to enter into a computer-generated realistic world where the users can interact with the world through sight and sound. The goal of VRT is to systematically expose people to a controlled and nonhazardous environment, but slowly expose the fearful individual to the fear-inducing stimulus while providing the individual strategies to cope with the stimulus. VRT is definitely more cost effective than exposing an individual to an actual audience on repeated occasions for the purpose of decreasing anxiety and is more realistic than having them imagine a public speaking occasion.

In a series of three different studies, VRT has been shown to be an effective means to help individuals reduce their fear of public speaking (it has not been tried on other forms of communication apprehension). In the first study, conducted by Slater, Pertaub, Barker, and Clark (2006), the researchers wanted to determine if the VR environment could actually induce anxiety within a set of highly communicative apprehensive participants. The researchers recruited both individuals with high levels of CA and low to average levels of CA. Ultimately, individuals with high levels of CA clearly experienced anxiety presenting a speech in front of a virtual audience more so than those individuals with low or moderate CA.

In a second study using virtual environments, Wallach, Safir, and Bar-Ziv (2009) compared traditional cognitive restructuring therapy to virtual cognitive restructuring therapy. In this study, the researchers purposefully recruited individuals who had acknowledged fears of public speaking. The researchers placed the participants into one of three groups: traditional therapy, virtual reality enhanced therapy, and a waitlist that functioned as a control group. In the first group, the participants went through a traditional cognitive behavioral therapeutic process, whereas in the virtual reality group they added the virtual audience exposure elements. Nothing happened to those individuals in the control group, but their levels of public speaking anxiety were measured. The therapeutic elements lasted for 12 weeks and consisted of 12 weekly sessions with a trained therapist. Both the traditional and VRT conditions were shown to be more effective at reducing public-speaking anxiety than a placebo, but the traditional and VRT conditions did not differ from each other. One difference that was noted, though, was the rate at which participants dropped out of the study. Twice as many individuals dropped out of the traditional cognitive behavioral condition as those who participated in the VRT condition.

In a final study conducted looking specifically at the use of VRT in public-speaking classrooms, North, Hill, Aikhuele, and North (2008) tested the utility of VRT as a tool for reducing public-speaking anxiety in a college classroom. Once again, the researchers found that the participants reported experiencing all of the same symptoms they would during a face-to-face public speaking occasion in the virtual world: dry mouth, nervousness, dizziness, sweating, shaking, and increased heart rate. During this study, the type of virtual auditorium the participants were exposed to changed. According to the study, here is the progression to which participants were exposed to the virtual auditorium:

- Speaking in an empty auditorium.
- Speaking in an auditorium with an audience.
- Speaking in an auditorium in which members talked to each other and paid no attention to speaker.
- Speaking to an audience whose members laughed at the speaker.
- Speaking to an audience in which members continuously asked the speaker to speak louder (p. 36).

Overall, after just five weekly sessions in the virtual public speaking auditorium, the researchers found a significant drop in the students' levels of public-speaking anxiety. Ultimately, using VRT could be a new tool for public-speaking teachers to help apprehensive students handle their public-speaking anxiety.

Skills Training

Unlike the two previously outlined treatment methods, which consist of generally accepted, formalized procedures, there are so many approaches to skills training it is difficult to outline what this method specifically includes or excludes. Programs labeled as "skills training" vary from a complete college course on communication skills to a few hours of training someone to call a person to ask for a date. Before we attempt to outline characteristics that a typical skills training program might include, we need to turn our attention to the general effectiveness of this approach.

We are familiar with the oldest and most widely used version of this treatment method: courses in speech or communication skills provided by high schools and colleges. In many instances, these courses are required of all students in the school or in a given major. Survey research conducted with adults in the United States suggests this form of skills training is almost wholly ineffective in reducing communication apprehension. In fact, our respondents regularly indicate that the course either has no effect on their level of apprehension about communication or makes it worse. We are not suggesting that high schools and colleges that require speech courses are intentionally trying to damage the high CA; in fact, many of these programs are instituted to help shy persons. The problem is that many times these programs don't help, they hurt. Hence, alternative communication classes need to be offered to assist the shy. Instead of public speaking or business and professional speaking as a requirement, schools could offer interpersonal or small group communication classes. The shy person can cope much easier with these courses and not learn to fear communication even more.

In contrast, numerous studies involving skills training for such specific goals as increasing assertiveness and learning to ask for a date have brought about major improvements in communication behavior, and at least a modest reduction in apprehension about the specific type of communication addressed in the treatment. Notably, in almost all of this research the subjects volunteered for treatment and were not required to participate. They identified themselves as skill deficient in the treatment area.

We believe the differences in the effects of these two divergent types of skills training stem from two factors. The first is the need for the willing cooperation of the person being treated. The second relates to the need for skills training to have narrowly defined targets for improvement.

As we noted previously, for any treatment program to be successful the recipient of the treatment must want to improve and be committed to following the advice of the professional helper. In the studies where skills training have been found to be most effective, the volunteer subjects had such a commitment. In contrast, data from our surveys of adults in the United States indicate that most of them only took the speech or communication skills courses because they were required to do so. The people who found the courses beneficial were primarily those who reported not having a high level of communication apprehension to begin with. Of the relatively small number who said they did have a high level of communication apprehension and the course helped reduce it, virtually all had voluntarily taken the course. These results suggest, therefore, the skills training programs that involve whole skills courses are not necessarily ineffective. Their lack of success might be due to the students who are in the program and either don't need it or don't want it.

The other factor distinguishing the two broad types of skills training programs relates to the definition of the target for improvement. Research in this area indicates the more narrowly the target behavior is defined, the greater the probability improvement will occur. In many skills-based courses the behaviors to be improved are poorly defined. "To present an effective speech" or "To conduct an employment interview" are no unusual statements of objectives in such courses. These are much too broad to be specific training targets. Although these may be general goals of such courses, for skills training to be effective these broad behavioral goals must be broken down to specific behaviors that can be identified and learned.

Before we look at skills training as an approach in helping people to reduce communication apprehension, we need to make clear the primary purpose of skills training: to improve skills. Thus, a skills-training program that can be demonstrated to improve skills should be judged successful, even if no impact on communication apprehension occurs. In some studies, this is the result that has been obtained. In others, some reduction in communication apprehension has also been observed.

Because skills training is time-consuming for both the professional helper and the person being treated, and thus tends to be expensive, its use as a method to help people reduce communication apprehension should be restricted to instances in which a true communication skills deficit actually exists. It is not enough that the people who are to receive treatment think they are skill deficient, they must actually be so. If they are adequately skilled, but think they aren't, the problem is one of inappropriate cognitive processing, and cognitive restructuring should be the treatment of choice. If they have deficient skills, but think their skills are satisfactory, no treatment is called for. Such individuals will lack the commitment to work with the professional helper, and consequently, no positive outcome is to be expected. One final word of caution concerning the use of skills training: Improved skills can be expected to result only in areas in which specific skills training is provided. By this we mean that skills training does not generalize. As an illustration, consider skills training for public speaking. If specific training in how to construct a good introduction to a speech is provided, we should expect the person after training to be able to prepare a better introduction. However, we should not expect the person to be able to prepare a better conclusion or to prepare better for a formal interview. Such skill generalization simply does not occur.

As a result, we cannot expect any generalized reduction in communication apprehension to be produced by skills training. To the extent that apprehension stems from deficient skills, with specific skills training we can expect to reduce only apprehension related to that particular skill area. Thus, skills training involving formal interviews might help reduce apprehension about communicating in interviews, but cannot be expected to reduce apprehension about communicating in any other communication context.

An effective skills training program normally includes the following components:

1. Identification of the specific skill deficiency (or deficiencies);
2. Determining subskills making up a larger area of deficient skill;
3. Establishing attainable goals for acquiring new skills;
4. Observing in an individual model the desirable skilled behavior to be learned;
5. Developing a cognitive understanding of the nature of the skill to be learned (becoming able to explain verbally what is to be done);
6. Practicing the new behavior in a controlled, nonthreatening environment where the helper can observe the behavior and suggest methods of improvement;
7. Practicing the new behavior in the natural environment.

Although not all skills-training programs include all of these components, most effective ones do. Many programs include other components as well. Sometimes the additional components are similar to cognitive restructuring in that they are directed toward creating a better understanding of the communication process and eliminating negative beliefs that might spawn negative self-statements.

Conclusions about Skills Training. Skills training as a method of reducing communication apprehension has limited usefulness. When a person has high communication apprehension about a variety of communication contexts, systematic desensitization or cognitive restructuring are the methods that should be used for treatment. If, however, the individual has high apprehension about only one type of communication context and has deficient skills in that area, skills training might be helpful.

Visualization

After many years of research and publications, Hopf and Ayres (1992) have concluded that visualization is an appropriate treatment method for reducing communication apprehension. We agree with their conclusion and are including some of their work in our text.

The theoretical basis for visualization was first introduced by Assagioli (1973, 1976). Ayres and Hopf (1991) have used visualization to lessen communication apprehension and improve communication performance in highly apprehensive individuals. Visualization is "a procedure that encourages people to think positively about public speaking by taking them through a carefully crafted script" (see Ayres & Hopf, 1989, for a sample script; Hopf & Ayres, 1992, p. 187).

A student uses visualization to picture the day of a presentation beginning full of energy and confidence and ending with a successful presentation. At the end of the visualization, the student is to congratulate himself on a job well done. Throughout the process the student is to practice relaxation and to think positively about each component of the process. The student is to visualize her or his success.

Conclusions about Visualization. Visualization should be used to help high apprehensive people build their confidence about public presentations (for more detailed information, see Ayres & Hopf, 1993).

Although complete implementation of the various treatments may take longer than the typical college course in public speaking, recent research by Duff, Levine, Beatty, Woolbright, and Park (2007) demonstrates some doubts in the effectiveness of systematic desensitization during a college public-speaking course. In the Duff et al. study, the researchers compared participants in three different conditions: a placebo group (participants were told they were listening to new age music containing hidden messages that would help reduce their anxiety on a tape), the first treatment group

Speaker speaking in an auditorium with audience

Photographee.eu/Shutterstock.com

(systematic desensitization tape created by Joe Ayres), the second treatment group (participants were exposed to three different types of treatment: visualization, skills based, and systematic desensitization), and a control group (nothing happened to these individuals). Ultimately, the reductions from either the first or second treatment groups were no better than those in the placebo group. In essence, neither the systematic desensitization group nor a combined therapeutic approach was any better than new age music.

Psychopharmacology

The final possible treatment for communication apprehension is really one designed for those individuals who have high levels of communication apprehension, have failed using the other treatment methods, and whose communication apprehension is negatively affecting their lives. Psychopharmacology is the study of how drugs alter an individual's moods, sensations, thinking patterns, and behaviors. As previously discussed in this book, the field of psychiatry has been examining aspects of public-speaking anxiety (and communication apprehension in general) in conjunction within the broader therapeutic concept of social phobia. In fact, many different psychiatric studies use public speaking as a method to induce social anxiety for determining the effectiveness of various treatments of social phobia as a distinct concept (Blöte, Kint, Miers, & Westenberg, 2009).

As a result of the psychiatric community's interest in social phobia, communication researchers recognize that a number of prescription medications are available to help some individuals reduce levels of public-speaking anxiety. However, as this is not a medical textbook, we do not want to spend a great deal of time going into the various treatment options. Instead, if you suffer from debilitating levels of communication apprehension and have tried the other methods of reducing your communication apprehension, you may want to seriously consider consulting with your primary care physician or a trained psychiatrist in what psychopharmacological options may be available for you. We should note, though, that, as with most medications, each psychopharmacological option is accompanied by various risks and side effects, so never enter into a medically based treatment program without being fully aware of those risks and possible side effects.

Summary

We stressed throughout this text that communication apprehension, communication avoidance, shyness, willingness to communicate, and communication effectiveness are all interrelated. Communication apprehension, whether generalized across communication contexts, specific to a given context, specific to a given receiver or group of receivers, or generated by a specific situation, is probably the single most important factor in causing ineffective communication.

A person who experiences communication apprehension is not the exception—almost all of us experience such apprehension at one time or another; some of us more often than others. For those of us who experience it only rarely, it is not a major problem in our lives. For those of us who experience it to the point that it interferes with our daily lives or stands in our way of personal or professional success, we need not accept this as something we have to endure.

As we noted in this chapter, communication apprehension can be substantially reduced by a variety of methods and has already been so reduced for literally thousands of individuals. Many schools and colleges have programs based on the methods discussed in this chapter available at little or no cost. Where no such program is available, except in low population areas, it is almost certain that a local clinical psychologist trained in the use of systematic desensitization and/or cognitive restructuring can provide the help needed. In addition, an increasing number of communication professors and specialists who can provide such help are making themselves available. The minimal cost of obtaining such help is far outweighed by the benefits obtained. If you feel you might benefit from such help, do not hesitate to seek it. Just like any other person with a problem (whether it be a fear of heights, spiders, flying, small spaces, large spaces, or fear of relationships), seek help to reduce your communication apprehension if you feel you need help and are willing to cooperate with the professional helper.

DISCUSSION QUESTIONS

1. The basic theories about why people experience fear or anxiety about communication is usually placed in three categories. What are these three categories, and how does each category have an impact on communication?
2. What is rhetoritherapy? When should it be used?
3. What is systematic desensitization? When should it be used?
4. What is cognitive restructuring? When should it be used?
5. What is skills training? When should it be used?
6. Who should administer SD? Cognitive restructuring? Skills training?
7. What is the success rate for systematic desensitization?
8. What are some examples of threatening situations used in SD?
9. Why is SD so successful with high communication apprehensives?

10. What is visualization? When should it be used?
11. If a person is apprehensive or anxious about communicating and wants help, what should he or she do?
12. What are your thoughts on using psychopharmacological interventions in a public-speaking course?

ACTIVITIES

1. Try the relaxation procedures listed in the text. Select a quiet, calm environment and relax each muscle group, starting with the hands and ending with the toes. After you have practiced the muscle-relaxation techniques, record how you feel at the end of the session. If you are the class instructor, take the students through the relaxation procedures, then ask each student to record those feelings.

2. In groups, compile a list of things that make you anxious, besides speaking in public. The list can include such things as insects, tests, and so on. Then compare lists and note how similar or dissimilar they are. Also note how many things people fear and how common it is to be anxious about a variety of situations.

3. Individually, compile a list of things you do well, from communication tasks to tasks at home or work. No matter how trivial the task seems, put it on the list. For example, you are a good cook, you do well in school, you play basketball well, you sew well, you sing well, you can change the oil in your car, and so on.

Glossary

Accidental Communication: When a source communicates a message to a receiver that is unintentional and happens outside the source's conscious control.

Adventurousness: Personality trait of someone who enjoys new experiences and tends to become bored with routine or repetitive matters.

Affinity Seeking: The degree to which we feel social needs for affection and inclusion; often manifests itself in our attempts to get other people to like and appreciate us.

Assertiveness: The capacity to make requests; actively disagree; express positive or negative personal rights and feelings; initiate, maintain, or disengage from conversations; and stand up for oneself without attacking another (factor of sociocommunicative orientation/style—see also responsiveness).

Audience Oriented Behavior: Personality characteristics that surface depending on the audience with whom an individual is communicating.

Channel: The means by which the message is conveyed from the source to the receiver.

Communication Apprehension: The fear or anxiety associated with either real or anticipated communication with another person or persons.

Communication Competence: The degree to which a person has the ability to make ideas known to others by talking or writing.

Contextual Behavior: When personality characteristics are demonstrated by individuals within specific contexts (interpersonal, group, meeting, public, and mediated).

Cultural Level of Communication: Adaptation of our message, message-sending and—receiving, processes occur to enable accurate predictions of our interactant's behavior based on her or his cultural background.

Decoding: Process a receiver goes through in sensing the source's message, interpreting it, evaluating it, and responding to it.

Encoding: Process a source goes through to create a message, adapt it to the receiver, and transmit it across some source-selected channel.

Ethnicity: Representing a classifying scheme that labels a group with similar geographical or cultural traditions

Expressive Communication: Messages sent by a source that expresses an internal emotional state.

Extraversion: The biologically based desire to be sociable, have stimulation around them, and have an easygoing nature.

Feedback: The receiver's response to the message after it has been seen or heard and then interpreted and evaluated.

General Anxiety: This personality trait distinguishes between those who tend to be tense, restless, and impatient most of the time, and those who generally tend to be calm, relaxed, and composed.

Human Communication: The process by which a person (or persons) stimulates meaning in the mind of another person (or persons) through the use of verbal and/or nonverbal messages.

Innovativeness: The personality characteristic that refers to a person's willingness to change or accept change in the society around them.

Intercultural Communication: Communication between members of two co-cultures within a larger culture, particularly when the co-culture differences as seen as quite substantial.

Interethnic Communication: Communication between members of more than one ethnic subculture.

Introversion: The biologically based desire to be shy and withdrawn with a preference to spending time alone.

Immediacy: The degree of perceived physical or psychological closeness between two people.

Message: Any verbal or nonverbal stimulus that might evoke meaning in the mind of the person receiving it.

Noise: Part of the rhetorical model of communication that is concerned with anything that prohibits effective rhetorical communication from occurring.

Neuroticism: Personality trait related to the biologically based tendency toward mania (being really happy) and depression (being really sad).

Pathological Behavior: When someone behaves and/or communicates abnormally to threatening situations.

Personality: A person's phenotype, or the interaction between an individual's genotype (see temperament) and her or his environment (nurture, diet, socialization, etc.), which is a reflection of her or his experiences, motivations, attitudes, beliefs, values, and behaviors.

Personality Traits: An individual's predispositions for responding in a certain way to various situations.

Psychological Level of Communication: Communicating with another person based on our predictions about how a person's beliefs, values, and behavior transcend cultural and social expectations and are derived from the person's unique psychological, emotional, and personality traits.

Receiver: The person (or persons) who receives the message.

Receiver Apprehension: The fear of misinterpreting, inadequately processing, and/or not being able to adjust psychologically to messages sent by others.

Religious Communication Apprehension: Anxiety or fear associated with either real or anticipated interaction about religion with people of other religions.

Responsiveness: The capacity to be sensitive to the communication of others, to be a good listener, to make others comfortable in communicating, and to recognize the needs and desires of others (factor of sociocommunicative orientation/style—see also assertiveness).

Rhetorical Communication: The process of a source specifically attempting to stimulate a particular meaning in the mind of the receiver by means of verbal and nonverbal messages.

Self-Control: A personality variable that separates people who have much control over their emotions from those who have little control over their emotions.

Self-Esteem: The view people have of themselves in terms of total worth.

Shyness: The behavioral tendency to not initiate communication and/or respond to the initiatives of others.

Singing Apprehension: A person's fear or anxiety about singing.

Situational Behavior: When personality characteristics surface for no reason; during a situation, we just naturally start communicating in a pattern that is not normal for us.

Sociological Level of Communication: Communicating with another person based on our predictions about other persons, which we use to make our encoding and decoding decisions that are based on our perceptions of the sociological subgroups to which people belong.

Source: The person (or persons) who originates a message.

Talkaholic (compulsive communicator): Personality trait in which individuals are driven to communicate.

Tolerance for Ambiguity: Personality variable that distinguishes people who can operate effectively in communication situations in which there is a great deal of uncertainty from those who cannot operate effectively in such situations.

Tolerance for Disagreement: An individual's ability to openly discuss opposition arguments to their own arguments without feeling personally attacked or confronted.

Uncertainty Reduction Theory: Theory that explains how individuals during interactions have a need to reduce uncertainty about others by gaining information about them.

Willingness to Communicate: A person's general level of desire to initiate communication with others.

Writing Apprehension: The fear or anxiety associated with writing situations.

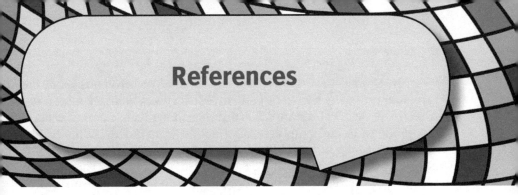

References

Andersen, P. A., Andersen, J. F., & Garrison, J. P. (1978). Singing apprehension and talking apprehension: The development of two constructs. *Sign Language Studies, 19*, 155–186.

Arias, V. S., Punyanunt-Carter, N. M., & Wrench, J. S. (2017). "I am spiritual, not religious": Examination of the Religious Receiver Apprehension Scale. *Journal of Communication & Religion, 39*, 72–91.

Assagioli, R. (1973). *The act of will*. New York: Viking Press.

Assagioli, R. (1976). *Psychosynthesis: A manual of principles and techniques*. New York: Penguin Books.

Ayres, J. (1989). The impact of communication apprehension and interaction structure on initial interactions. *Communication Monographs, 56*, 75–86.

Ayres, J., & Hopf, T. S. (1985). Visualization: A means of reducing speaking anxiety. *Communication Education, 34*, 318–323.

Ayres, J., & Hopf, T. S. (1987). Visualization, systematic desensitization, and rational-emotive therapy: A comparative evaluation. *Communication Education, 36*, 236–240.

Ayres, J., & Hopf, T. S. (1989). Visualization: Is it more than extra-attention? *Communication Education, 38*, 1–5.

Ayres, J., & Hopf, T. S. (1991). Visualization: Reducing speaking anxiety and enhancing performance. *Communication Reports, 5*, 1–10.

Ayres, J., & Hopf, T. S. (1993). *Coping with speech anxiety*. Norwood, NJ: Ablex Publishing.

Arquero, J. L., Hassall, T. J., Joyce, J., & Donoso, J. A. (2007) Accounting students and communication apprehension: A Study of Spanish and UK Students. *European Accounting Review, 16*, 299–322. doi:10.1080/09638180701391337

Bandura, A. (1977). Self-efficacy: Toward a unifying theory of behavior and behavior change. *Psychological Review, 84*, 191–215.

Bandura, A., Blanchard, E. B., & Ritter B. (1969). The relative efficacy of desensitization and modeling approaches for inducing behavioral, affective, and attitudinal change. *Journal of Personality and Social Psychology, 13*, 173–199.

Barker, L., Cegala, D. J. Kibler, Wahlers, K. J. (1972). Hypnosis and the reduction of speech anxiety. *Central States Speech Journal, 23,* 28–35.

Bartoo, H., & Sias. P. (2004). When enough is too much: Communication apprehension and employee information experiences. *Communication Quarterly, 51,* 15–26.

Bashore, D. N., McCroskey, J. C., & Andersen, J. F. (1976). The relationship between communication apprehension and academic achievement among college students. *Human Communication Research, 3,* 73–81.

Beatty, M. J. (1984). Physiological assessment. In J. A. Daly and J. C. McCroskey (Eds.), *Avoiding communication: Shyness, reticence, and communication apprehension* (pp. 95–106). Beverly Hills, CA: Sage.

Beatty, M. J., & Behnke, R. R. (1980). An assimilation theory perspective of communication apprehension. *Human Communication Research, 6,* 319–325.

Beatty, M. J., & Dobos, J. A. (1992). Adult sons' satisfaction with their relationship with fathers and person-group (father) communication apprehension. *Communication Quarterly, 40,* 162–176.

Beatty, M. J., & Dobos, J. A. (1993). Adult males' perceptions of confirmation and relational partner communication apprehension: Indirect effects of fathers on sons' partners. *Communication Quarterly, 41,* 66–76.

Beatty, M. J., Dobos, J. A., Balfantz, G. L., & Kuwabara, A. Y. (1991). Communication apprehension, state anxiety, and behavioral disruption: A causal analysis. *Communication Quarterly, 39,* 48–57.

Beatty, M. J., Heisel, A. D., Lewis, R. J., Pence, M. E., Reinhart, A., & Tian, Y. (2011). Communication apprehension and resting alpha range asymmetry in the anterior cortex. *Communication Education, 60,* 441–460. doi: 10.1080/03634523.2011.563389

Beatty, M. J., McCroskey, J. C., & Floyd, K. (Eds.). (2009). *Biological dimensions of communication: Perspectives, methods, and research.* Cresskill, NJ: Hampton Press.

Beatty, M. J., McCroskey, J. C., & Heisel, A.D. (1998). Communication apprehension as temperamental expression: A communibiological paradigm. *Communication Monographs, 65,* 197–219.

Beatty, M. J., & McCroskey, J. C., & Valencic, K. M. (2001). *The biology of communication: A communibiological perspective.* Cresskill, NJ: Hampton Press.

Behnke, R. R., & Beatty, M. J. (1981). A cognitive-physiological model of speech anxiety. *Communication Monographs, 48,* 158–163.

Bell, R. A, & Daly, J. A. (1984). The affinity-seeking function of communication. *Communication Monographs,* 51, 91–115. Bern, S. L. (1974). The measurement of psychological androgyny. *Journal of Consulting and Clinical Psychology, 42,* 155–162.

Bem, S. L. (1974). The measurement of psychological androgyny. *Journal of Consulting and Clinical Psychology, 47,* 155–162.

Berger, B. A., McCroskey, J. C., & Richmond, V. P. (1984). Communication apprehension and shyness. In W. N. Tindall, R. S. Beardsley, & F. R. Curtiss (Eds.), *Communication in pharmacy practice: A practical guide for students and practitioners* (pp. 128–158). Philadelphia, PA: Lea and Febiger.

Berger, C. R., & Calabrese, R. J. (1975). Some explorations in initial interaction. Toward a developmental theory of interpersonal communication. *Human Communication Research, 1,* 99–112.

Berlo, D. K. (1960). *The process of communication.* New York: Holt, Rinehart & Winston.

Bippus, A. M., & Dorjee, T. (2002). The validity of the RECA as an index of interethnic communication apprehension. *Communication Research Reports, 19,* 130–137.

Blöte, A. W., Kint, M. W., Miers, A. C., & Westenberg, P. (2009). The relation between public speaking anxiety and social anxiety: A review. *Journal of Anxiety Disorders, 23,* 305–313. doi:10.1016/j.janxdis.2008.11.007

Bolls, P. D., & Tan, A. (1996). Communication anxiety and teacher communication competence among Native American and Caucasian students. *Communication Research Reports, 13,* 205–213.

Boorom, M. L., Goolsby, J. R., & Ramsey, R. P. (1998). Relational communication traits and their effect on adaptiveness and sales performance. *Journal of the Academy of Marketing Science, 26,* 16–30.

Booth-Butterfield, S. (1988). The effect of communication apprehension and anticipated interaction on student recall of information. Dissertation completed at West Virginia University.

Booth-Butterfield, M., & Booth-Butterfield, S. (1991). The effect of communication anxiety upon signing effectiveness among the profoundly hearing-impaired. *Communication Quarterly, 39,* 241–250.

Booth-Butterfield, M., & Booth-Butterfield, S. (1993). The role of cognitive performance orientation in communication anxiety. *Communication Quarterly, 41,* 198–209.

Booth-Butterfield, S., Chory, R., & Beynon, W. (1997). Communication apprehension and health communication and behaviors. *Communication Quarterly, 45,* 235–250.

Bourhis, J., Allen, M., & Bauman, I. (2006). Communication apprehension: Issues to consider in the classroom. In B. M. Gayle, R. W. Preiss, N. Burrell, & M. Allen's (Eds.), *Classroom communication and instructional processes: Advances through meta-analysis* (pp. 211–227). Mahwah, NJ: Lawrence Erlbaum.

Burgoon, J. K. (1976). The unwillingness-to-communicate scale: Development and validation. *Communication Monographs, 43,* 60–69.

Buss, A. H. (1980). *Self-consciousness and social anxiety.* San Francisco: W. H. Freeman.

Buss, A. H. (1984). A conception of shyness. In J. A. Daly & J. C. McCroskey (Eds.), *Avoiding communication: Shyness, reticence, and communication apprehension* (pp. 39–50). Beverly Hills, CA: Sage.

Butler, J., Pryor, B., & Marti, S. (2004). Communication apprehension and honors students. *North American Journal of Psychology, 6,* 293–296.

Carmack, H. J., & DeGroot, J. M. (2016). Development and validation of the Communication Apprehension About Death Scale. *OMEGA—Journal of Death and Dying, 74,* 239–259. doi: 10.1177/0030222815598440

Cheek, J. M., & Busch, C. M. (1981). The influence of shyness on loneliness in a new situation. *Personality and Social Psychology Bulletin, 7,* 572–577.

Clevenger, T., Jr. (1959). A synthesis of experimental research in stage fright. *Quarterly Journal of Speech, 45,* 134–145.

Colby, N., Hopf, T., & Ayres, J. (1993). Nice to meet you? Inter/Intra personal perceptions of communication apprehension in initial interactions. *Communication Quarterly, 41,* 221–230.

Cole, J. G., & McCroskey, J. C. (2003). The association of perceived communication apprehension, shyness, and verbal aggression with perceptions of source credibility and affect in organizational and interpersonal contexts. *Communication Quarterly, 51,* 101–110.

Cortese, J., & Seo, M. (2012). The role of social presence in opinion expression during FtF and CMC discussions. *Communication Research Reports, 29,* 44–53. doi: 10.1080/08824096.2011.639913

Croucher, S. M., Sommier, M., Rahmani, D., & Appenrodt, J. (2015). A cross-cultural analysis of communication apprehension. *Journal of Intercultural Communication, 38.* Retrieved from: https://www.immi.se/intercultural/

Daly, J. A., & Hailey, J. L. (1983). Putting the situation into writing research: Situation parameters of writing apprehension as disposition and state. In R. E. Beach & L. Bidwell (Eds.), *New directions in composition research.* New York: Guilford.

Daly, J. A., & McCroskey, J. C. (Eds.). (1984). *Avoiding communication: Shyness, reticence, and communication apprehension.* Beverly Hills, CA: Sage.

Daly, J. A., McCroskey, J. C., Ayres, J., Hopf, T., Ayres Sonandré, D. M., & Wongprasert, T. K. (2009). *Avoiding communication: Shyness, reticence, and communication apprehension* (3rd ed.). Cresskill, NK: Hampton Press.

Daly, J. A., & Miller, M. D. (1975). The empirical development of an instrument to measure writing apprehension. *Research in the Teaching of English, 9,* 242–249.

Daly, J. A., McCroskey, J. C., & Richmond, V. P. (1977). The relationships between vocal activity and perception of communicators in small group interaction. *Western Speech Communication Journal, 41,* 175–187.

Daly, J. A., Richmond, V. P., & Leth, S. (1979). Social communication anxiety and the personnel selection process: Testing the similarity effect in selection decisions. *Human Communication Research, 6,* 18–32.

Duff, D. C., Levine, T. R., Beatty, M. J., Woolbright, J. & Park, H. S. (2007). Testing public anxiety treatments against a credible placebo control. *Communication Education, 56,* 72–88. doi: 10.1080/03634520601016186

Ellis, A. (1962). *Reason and emotion in psychotherapy.* New York: Stuart.

Ericson, P. M., & Gardner, J. W. (1992). Two longitudinal studies of communication apprehension and its effects on college students' success. *Communication Quarterly, 40,* 127–137.

Eysenck, H. J. (1970). *Readings in extraversion-introversion* (Vol. 1). New York: Wiley-Interscience.

Eysenck, H. J. (1971). *Readings in extraversion-introversion* (Vol. II). New York: Wiley-Interscience.

Eysenck, H. J. (1998). *Dimensions of personality* (rev. ed.). New Brunswick, NJ: Transaction.

Freimuth, V. S. (1982). Communication apprehension in the classroom. In L. Barker (Ed.), *Communication in the classroom.* Englewood Cliffs, NJ: Prentice-Hall.

Fremouw, W. J. (1984). Cognitive-behavioral therapies for modification of communication apprehension. In J. A. Daly & J. C. McCroskey (Eds.), *Avoiding communication: Shyness, reticence, and communication apprehension* (pp. 209–218). Beverly Hills, CA: Sage.

Gilkinson, H. (1942). Social fears as reported by students in college speech classes. *Speech Monographs, 9,* 141–160.

Gorham, J. (1988). The relationship between verbal teacher immediacy behaviors and student learning. *Communication Education, 37,* 40–53.

Goss, B., Thompson, M., & Olds, S. (1978). Behavioral support for systematic desensitization for communication apprehension. *Human Communication Research, 4,* 158–163.

Gudykunst, W. B., & Kim, Y. Y. (2002). *Communicating with strangers: An approach to intercultural communication* (4th ed.). New York, NY: McGraw-Hill.

Hackman, M. Z., & Barthel-Hackman, T. A. (1993). Communication apprehension, willingness to communication, and sense of humor: United States and New Zealand perspectives. *Communication Quarterly, 41*(3), 282–291.

Hammick, J. K., & Lee, M. J. (2014). Do shy people feel less communication apprehension online? The effects of virtual reality on the relationship between personality characteristics and communication outcomes. *Computers in Human Behavior, 33*, 302–310. doi: 10.1016/j.chb.2013.01.046

Hashemi, Z., Hadavi, M., & Valinejad, M. (2016). Communication apprehension and fear of physician in the patients referring to the clinics of Rafsanjan. *Medical Ethics Journal, 10*, 37–47.

Hays, D. P., & Meltzer, L. (1972). Interpersonal judgments based on talkativeness: Fact or artifact? *Sociometry, 33*, 538–561.

Hoffman, J., & Sprague, J. (1982). A survey of reticence and communication apprehension treatment programs at U.S. colleges and universities. *Communication Education, 31*, 185–193.

Hofstede, G., & Hofstede, G. J. (2005). *Cultures and organizations: Software of the mind–Intercultural cooperation and its importance for survival* (rev. ed.). New York, NY: McGraw-Hill.

Hopf, T., & Ayres, J., (1992), Coping with public speaking anxiety: An examination of various combinations of systematic desensitization, skills training, and visualization. *Journal of Applied Communication Research, 20*, 184–198.

Hsu, C. F. (1998). Relations between family characteristics and communication apprehension. *Communication Research Reports, 15*, 91–98.

Hsu, C. F. (2010). Acculturation and communication traits: A study of cross-cultural adaptation among Chinese in America. *Communication Monographs, 77*, 414–425. doi: 10.1080/03637751.2010.499367

Hutchinson, K. L., & Neuliep, J. W. (1993). The influence of parent and peer modeling on the development of communication apprehension in elementary school children. *Communication Quarterly, 41*, 16–25.

Jacobson, E. (1938). *Progressive relaxation.* Chicago: University of Chicago Press.

Jung, H. Y., & McCroskey, J. C. (2004). Communication apprehension in a first language and self-perceived competence as predictors of communication apprehension in a second language: A study of speakers of English as a second language. *Communication Quarterly, 52*, 170–181.

Kido, K., Kim, M. S., Sur, J., Hendrickson, B., & Doi, R. (2008, November). *The relationship between individual characteristics and attitudes toward humanoid robots in human-robot communication.* Paper presented at the National Communication Association Convention. San Diego, CA.

Kim, M. (2002). *Non-Western perspectives on human communication: Implications for theory and practice.* Thousand Oaks, CA: Sage.

Klopf, D. W. (1984). Cross-cultural apprehension research: A summary of Pacific Basin studies. In J. A. Daly & J. C. McCroskey (Eds.), *Avoiding communication: Shyness, reticence, and communication apprehension* (pp. 157–172). Beverly· Hills, CA: Sage.

Klopf, D. W. (1984). Cross-cultural apprehension research: Procedures and comparisons. In J. A. Daly, J. C. McCroskey, J. Ayres, T. Hopf, & D. M. Ayres (Eds.), *Avoiding communication: Shyness, reticence, and communication apprehension* (2nd ed., pp. 269–284). Cresskill, NJ: Hampton Press.

Klopf, D. W. (2009). Cross-cultural communication apprehension research. In J. A. Daly, J. C. McCroskey, J. Ayres, T. Hopf, D. M. Ayres Sonandre, & T. K. Wongprasert (Eds.), *Avoiding communication: Shyness, reticence, and communication apprehension* (3rd ed., pp. 241–253). Cresskill, NJ: Hampton Press.

Krishman, A., & Atkin, D. (2014). Individual differences in social networking site users: The interplay between antecedents and consequential effect on level of activity. *Computers in Human Behavior, 40*, 111–118. doi: 10.1016/j.chb.2014.07.045

Lashbrook, W. B., Knutson, P. K., Parsley, M. L., & Wenburg, J. R. (1976 November). *An empirical examination of versatility as a consequent of perceived social style.* Paper presented at the annual convention of the Western States Speech Communication Association, Phoenix, AZ.

Lin, Y., & Rancer, A. S. (2003). Ethnocentrism, intercultural communication apprehension, intercultural willingness-to-communicate, and intentions to participate in an intercultural dialogue program: Testing a proposed model. *Communication Research Reports, 20*, 62–72.

Lucchetti, A. E., Powers, W. G., Love, D. E. (2002). The empirical development of child–parent communication apprehension scale for use with young adults. *The Journal of Family Communication, 2*, 109–131.

Malachowski, C. C., Martin, M. W., & Vallade, J. I. (2013). An examination of students' adaptation, aggression, and apprehension traits with their instructional feedback orientations. *Communication Education, 62*, 127–147. doi: 10.1080/03634523.2012.748208

Martini, M., Behnke, R. R, & King, P. E. (1992). The communication of public speaking anxiety: Perceptions of Asian and American speakers. *Communication Quarterly, 40*, 279–288.

McCroskey, J. C. (1970). Measures of communication-bound anxiety. *Speech Monographs, 37*, 269–277.

McCroskey, J. C. (1972). The implementation of a large-scale program of systematic desensitization for communication apprehension. *Speech Teacher, 21*, 255–264.

McCroskey, J. C. (1977). Classroom consequences of communication apprehension: *Communication Education, 26*, 27–33.

McCroskey, J. C. (1977). Oral communication apprehension: A summary of recent theory and research. *Human Communication Research, 4,* 78–96.

McCroskey, J. C. (1977). *Quiet children and the classroom teacher.* Urbana, IL: Educational Resources Information Center.

McCroskey, J. C. (1978). Validity of the PRCA as an index of oral communication apprehension. *Communication Monographs, 45,* 192–203.

McCroskey, J. C. (1980). On communication competence and communication apprehension: A response to page. *Communication Education, 29,* 109–111.

McCroskey, J. C. (1980). Quiet children in the classroom: On helping not hurting. *Communication Education, 29,* 239–244.

McCroskey, J. C. (1982). Oral communication apprehension: A reconceptualization. In M. Burgoon (Ed.), *Communication Yearbook,* 6 (pp. 136–170). Beverly Hills, CA: Sage.

McCroskey, J. C. (1984). The communication apprehension perspective. In J. A. Daly & J. C. McCroskey (Eds.), *Avoiding communication: Shyness, reticence, and communication apprehension* (pp. 13–38). Beverly Hills, CA: Sage.

McCroskey, J. C. (1984). Self-report measurement. In J. A. Daly & J. C. McCroskey (Eds.), *Avoiding communication: Shyness, reticence, and communication apprehension* (pp. 81–94). Beverly Hills, CA: Sage.

McCroskey, J. C. (1992). Reliability and validity of the willingness to communicate scale. *Communication Quarterly, 40,* 16–25.

McCroskey, J. C., Daly, J. A., Martin, M. M., & Beatty, M. J. (Eds.) (1998). *Communication and personality: Trait perspectives.* Cresskill, NJ: Hampton Press.

McCroskey, J. C., Fayer, J. M., & Richmond, V. P. (1985). Don't speak to me in English: Communication apprehension in Puerto Rico. *Communication Quarterly, 33,* 185–192.

McCroskey, J. C., & McCroskey, L. L. (1986). *Self-report as an approach to measuring communication competence.* Paper presented at the annual convention of the Central States Speech Communication Association, Cincinnati, OH.

McCroskey, J. C., & Richmond, V. P. (1978). Community size as a predictor of development of communication apprehension: Replication and extension. *Communication Education, 27,* 212–219.

McCroskey, J. C., & Richmond, V. P. (1979). The impact of communication apprehension on individuals in organizations. *Communication Quarterly, 27,* 55–66.

McCroskey, J. C., & Richmond, V. P. (1980). *The quiet ones: Shyness and communication apprehension.* Scottsdale, AZ: Gorsuch Scarisbrick.

McCroskey, J. C., & Richmond, V. P. (1982). *The quiet ones: Communication apprehension and shyness,* 2nd oo. Scottsdale, AZ: Gorsuch Scarisbrick.

McCroskey, J. C., & Richmond, V. P. (1987). Willingness to communicate. In J. C. McCroskey & J. A. Daly (Eds.), *Personality and interpersonal communication.* (pp. 129–156). Beverly Hills, CA: Sage.

McCroskey, J. C., & Richmond, V. P. (1988). Communication apprehension and small group communication. In R. S. Cathcart & L. A. Samovar (Eds.), *Small group communication: A reader* (5th ed., pp. 405–420). Dubuque, Iowa: Wm. C. Brown.

McCroskey, J. C., & Richmond, V. P. (1990). Willingness to communicate: Differing cultural perspectives. *The Southern Communication Journal, 56,* 72–77.

McCroskey, J. C., & Richmond, V. P. (1991). *Quiet children in the classroom* (2nd ed.). Urbana, IL: Educational Resources Information Center.

McCroskey, J. C., & Richmond, V. P. (1992). *Introduction to interpersonal communication.* Edina, MN: Burgess International Group.

McCroskey, J. C., & Richmond, V. P. (1993). Identifying compulsive communicators: The talkaholic scale. *Communication Research Reports, 10,* 107–114.

McCroskey, J. C., & Richmond, V. P. (1998). Willingness to communicate, In J. C. McCroskey, J. A. Daly, M. M. Martin, & M. J. Beatty (Eds.), *Communication and personality: Trait perspectives* (pp. 119–132). Cresskill, NJ: Hampton Press.

McCroskey, J. C., & Richmond, V. P. (2006). Understanding the audience: Students' communication traits. In T. P. Mottet, V. P. Richmond, & J. C. McCroskey's (Eds.), *Handbook of instructional communication: Rhetorical & relational perspectives* (pp. 51–66). Boston: Pearson/ Allyn & Bacon.

McCroskey, J. C., & Wheeless, L. R. (1976). *Introduction to human communication.* Boston: Allyn and Bacon.

McCroskey, J. C., Fayer, J., & Richmond, V. P. (1985). Don't speak to me in English: Communication apprehension among Puerto Rican students. *Communication Quarterly, 33,* 185–192.

McCroskey; J. C., Larson, C. R, & Knapp, M. L. (1971). *An introduction to interpersonal communication.* Englewood Cliffs, NJ: Prentice-Hall.

McCroskey, J. C., Ralph, D. C., & Barrick, J. E. (1968, December). *The effect of systematic desensitization on speech anxiety.* Paper presented at the annual convention of the Speech Association of America, Chicago, IL.

McCroskey, J. C., Ralph, D. C., & Barrick, J. E. (1970). The effect of systematic desensitization on speech anxiety. *Speech Teacher, 19,* 32–36.

McCroskey, J. C., Richmond, V. P., & Stewart, R. (1986). *One-on-one: The foundations of interpersonal communication*. Englewood Cliffs, NJ: Prentice-Hall.

McCroskey, J. C., Andersen, J. F., Richmond, V. P., & Wheeless, L. R. (1981). Communication apprehension of elementary and secondary students and teachers. *Communication Education, 30,* 122–132.

McCroskey, J. C., Burroughs, N. E, Daun, A., & Richmond, V. P. (1990). Correlates of quietness: Swedish and American perspectives. *Communication Quarterly, 38,* 127–137.

McCroskey, J. C., Richmond, V. P., Berger, B. A., & Baldwin, H. J. (1983). How to make a good thing worse: A comparison of approaches to helping students overcome communication apprehension. *Communication, 12,* 213–220.

McCroskey, J. C., Daly, J. A., Richmond, V. P., & Cox, B. (1975). The effects of communication apprehension on interpersonal attraction. *Human Communication Research, 2,* 51–65.

McCroskey, J. C., Richmond, V. P., Daly, J. A., & Falcione, R. L. (1977). Studies of the relationship between communication apprehension and self-esteem. *Human Communication Research, 3,* 269–277.

McCroskey, J. C., Wrench, J. S., & Richmond, V. P. (2003). *Principles of public speaking*. Indianapolis, IN: The College Network.

Mehrabian, A. (1971). *Silent messages*. Belmont, CA: Wadsworth.

Meichenbaum, D. (1977). *Cognitive behavior modification*. New York: Plenum.

Merrill, D. W., & Reid, R. (1981). *Personal styles and effective performance: Make your style work for you*. Radnor, PA: Chilton Book.

Miller, O. R., & Steinberg, M. (1975). *Between people: A new analysis of interpersonal communication*. Chicago: Science Research Associates.

Mortensen, D. C., Arntson, P. H., & Lustig, M. (1977). The measurement of verbal predispositions: Scale development and application. *Human Communication Research, 3,* 146–158.

Nass, C., & Yen, C. (2010). *The man who lied to his laptop: What machines tech us about human relationships*. New York, NY: Current.

Neuliep, J. W., & McCroskey, J. C. (1997). The development of the intercultural and interethnic communication apprehension scales. *Communication Research Reports, 14,* 145–156.

Neuliep, J. W., & Ryan, D. J. (1998). The influence of intercultural communication apprehension and socio-communicative orientation on uncertainty reduction during initial cross-cultural interaction. *Communication Quarterly, 46,* 88–99.

Newton, C. K. (1986). *The social style profile: A perspective on its development*. Denver, CO: The TRACOM Corporation/A Reed Publishing USA Company.

Nomura, T., Suzuki, T., Kanda, T., & Kato, K. (2006). Measurement of anxiety toward robots. Robot and Human Interactive Communication, In *Proc. the 15th IEEE International Symposium on Robot and Human Interactive Communication (RO-MAN)*, 372–377.

North, M. H., Hill, J., Aikhuele, A. S., & North, S. M. (2008). Virtual reality training in aid of communication apprehension in classroom environments. *International Journal of Educational Technology, 3*, 34–37.

Öhman, A. (2009). Of snakes and faces: An evolutionary perspective on the psychology of fear. *Scandinavian Journal of Psychology, 50*, 543–552. doi:10.1111/j.1467-9450.2009.00784.x

Paul, G. L. (1966). *Insight vs. desensitization in psychotherapy: An experiment in anxiety reduction*. Stanford, CA: Stanford University Press.

Payne, S. K., & Richmond, V. P. (1984). A bibliography of related theory and research. In J. A. Daly & J. C. McCroskey (Eds.), *Avoiding communication: Shyness, reticence, and communication apprehension*. Beverly Hills, CA: Sage.

Perrault, E. K., & Silk, K. J. (2015). Reducing communication apprehension for new patients through information found within physicians' biographies. *Journal of Health Communication, 20*, 743–750. doi: 10.1080/10810730.2015.1018569

Phillips, G. M. (1968). Reticence: Pathology of the normal speaker. *Speech Monographs, 35*, 39–49.

Phillips, O. M. (1977). Rhetoritherapy versus the medical model: Dealing with reticence. *Communication Education, 26*, 34–43.

Phillips, G. M. (1981). *Help for shy people and anyone else who ever felt ill at ease on entering a room full of strangers*. Englewood Cliffs, NJ: Prentice-Hall.

Phillips, O. M. (1991). *Communication incompetencies: A theory of training oral performance behavior*. Carbondale and Edwardsville: Southern Illinois University Press.

Pilkonis, P., Heape, C., & Klein, R. H. (1980). Treating shyness and other relationship difficulties in psychiatric outpatients. *Communication Education, 29*, 250–255.

Powers, W. G., & Love, D. E. (2000). Communication apprehension in the dating partner context. *Communication Research Reports, 17*, 221–228.

Punyanunt-Carter, N. M., Corrigan, M. W., Wrench, J. S., & McCroskey, J. C. (2010). Examining forbidden dinner conversation topics: A quantitative analysis of political affiliation, religiosity, and religious-based communication. *Journal of Communication and Religion, 33*, 1–32.

Punyanunt-Carter, N. M., De La Cruz, J. J., & Wrench, J. S. (2017). Investigating the relationships among college students' satisfaction, addiction, needs, communication apprehension, motives, and uses & gratifications with Snapchat. *Computers in Human Behavior, 75,* 870–875. doi: 10.1016/j.chb.2017.06.034

Punyanunt-Carter, N. M., Wrench, J. C., Corrigan, M. W., & McCroskey, J. C. (2008). An examination of reliability and validity of the Religious Communication Apprehension Scale. *Journal of Intercultural Communication Research, 37,* 1–15. doi: 10.1080/174757080277339

Richmond, V. P. (1978). The relationship between trait and state communication apprehension and interpersonal perception during acquaintance stages. *Human Communication Research, 4,* 338–349.

Richmond, V. P. (1980). Monomorphic and polymorphic opinion leadership within a relatively closed communication system. *Human Communication Research, 6,* 111–116.

Richmond, V. P. (1984). Implications of quietness: Some facts and speculations. In J. A. Daly & J. C. McCroskey (Eds.), *Avoiding communication: Shyness, reticence, and communication apprehension* (pp. 145–156). Beverly Hills, CA: Sage.

Richmond, V. P., & McCroskey, J. C. (1990). Reliability and separation of factors on the assertiveness-responsiveness measure. *Psychological Reports, 67,* 449–450.

Richmond, V. P., McCroskey, J. C., McCroskey, L. L., & Fayer, J. M. (2008). Communication traits in first and second languages: Puerto Rico. *Journal of Intercultural Communication Research, 37,* 64–73. doi:10.1080/1747570802533331

Richmond, V. P., & Roach, K. D. (1992). Willingness to communicate and employee success in U. S. organizations. *Journal of Applied Communication Research, 20,* 95–115.

Richmond, V. P., Beatty, M., & Dyba, P. (1985). Shyness and popularity: Children's views. *Western Speech Communication Journal, 49,* 116–125.

Richmond, V. P., Gorham, J. S., & Furio, B. J. (1987). Affinity-seeking communication in collegiate female–male relationships. *Communication Quarterly, 35,* 334–348.

Richmond, V. P., Gorham, J. S., & McCroskey, J. C. (1987). The relationship between selected immediacy behaviors and cognitive learning. In M. McLaughlin (Ed.), *Communication Yearbook 10* (pp. 574–590). Beverly Hills, CA: Sage.

Richmond, V. P., McCroskey, J. C., & Davis, L. M. (1986). Communication apprehension and affinity-seeking in superior-subordinate relationships. *World Communication, 15,* 41–54.

Richmond, V. P., McCroskey, J. C., & Davis, L. M. (1986). The relationship of supervisor use of power and affinity-seeking strategies with subordinate satisfaction. *Communication Quarterly, 34*, 178–193.

Richmond, V. P., McCroskey, J. C., & Payne, S. K. (1991). *Nonverbal behavior in interpersonal relationships* (2nd ed.). Englewood Cliffs, NJ: Prentice-Hall.

Richmond, V. P., Smith, R. S., Jr., Heisel, A. D., & McCroskey, J. C. (1998). The impact of communication apprehension and fear of talking with a physician and perceived medical outcomes. *Communication Research Reports, 15*, 344–353.

Richmond, V. P., Smith, R. S., Jr., Heisel, A. D., & McCroskey, J. C. (2001). Nonverbal immediacy in the physician/patient relationship. *Communication Research Reports, 18*, 211–216.

Seligman, M. E. P. (1970). On the generality of the laws of learning. *Psychological Review, 77*, 406–418.

Seligman, M. E. P. (1971). Phobias and preparedness. *Behavior Therapy, 2*, 307–320.

Shannon, C. E., & Weaver, W. (1949). *The mathematical theory of communication.* Urbana, IL: University of Illinois Press.

Siegel, M. (2005, December). Can we cure FEAR? *Scientific American Mind, 16*(4), 44–49.

Slater, M., Pertaub, D. P., Barker, C., & Clark, D. M. (2006). An experimental study on fear of public speaking using a virtual environment. *Cyberpsychology & Behavior, 9*, 627–633.

Sorensen, G. (1972). *The use of personality traits and communication apprehension in predicting interaction behavior in small groups.* Master's thesis, Illinois State University.

Sorensen, G., and McCroskey, J. C. (1977). The prediction of interaction behavior 'in small groups: Zero history vs. intact groups. *Communication Monographs, 44*, 73–80.

Spielberger, C. D. (Ed.) (1966). *Anxiety and behavior.* New York: Academic Press.

Spielberger, C. D. (1966). Theory and research on anxiety. In C. D. Spielberger (Ed.), *Anxiety and behavior* (pp. 3–20). New York: Academic Press.

Stockstill, C. J., & Roach, K. D. (2007). Communication apprehension in high school students. *Texas Speech Communication Journal, 32*, 53–64.

Tillfors, M., Furmark, T., Marteinsdottir, I., Fischer, H., Pissiota, A., Långström, B., & Fredrikson, M. (2001). Cerebral blood flow in subjects with social phobia during stressful speaking tasks: A PET study. *American Journal of Psychiatry, 158*, 1220–1226.

Tjosvold, D., Hui, C., & Sun, H. (2000). Social face and open-mindedness: Constructive conflict in Asia. In C. M. Lau, C. S. Wong, K. K. S. Law, & D. K. Tse (Eds.), *Asian management matters: Regional relevance and global impact* (pp. 3–16). London, England: Imperial College Press.

Toale, M. C., & McCroskey, J. C. (2001). Ethnocentrism and trait communication apprehension as predictors of interethnic communication apprehension and use of relational maintenance strategies in interethnic communication. *Communication Quarterly, 49,* 70–83.

Wallach, H. S., Safir, M. P., & Bar-Ziv, M. (2009). Virtual reality cognitive behavior therapy for public speaking anxiety: A randomized clinical trial. *Behavior Modification, 33,* 314–338.

Watzlawik, T., Beavin, J., & Jackson, D. D. (1967). *Pragmatics of human communication.* New York: W. W. Norton.

Wheeless, V. (1984). Communication apprehension and trust as predictors of willingness to discuss gynecological health topics. *Communication Research Reports, 1,* 117–121.

Wheeless, V. E., & Dierks-Stewart, K. (1981). The psychometric properties of the Bem Sex-Role Inventory: Questions concerning reliability and validity. *Communication Quarterly, 29,* 173–186.

Wolpe, J. (1958). *Psychotherapy by reciprocal inhibition.* Stanford, CA: Stanford· University Press.

Wrench, J. S., McCroskey, J. C., & Richmond, V. P. (2008). *Human communication in everyday life: Explanations and applications.* Boston, MA: Allyn & Bacon.

Wrench, J. S., Corrigan, M. W., McCroskey, J. C., & Punyanunt-Carter N. M. (2006). Religious fundamentalism and intercultural communication: The relationships among ethnocentrism, intercultural communication apprehension, religious fundamentalism, homonegativity, and tolerance for religious disagreements. *Journal of Intercultural Communication Research, 35,* 23–44. doi: 10.1080/17457406007391 98

Wrench, J. S., & Punyanunt-Carter, N. M. (2007). The relationship between computer-mediated communication competence, apprehension, self-efficacy, perceived confidence, and social presence. *Southern Communication Journal, 72,* 355–378. doi: 10.1080/10417940701667696

Wrench, J. S., Thomas-Maddox, C., Richmond, V. P., & McCroskey, J. C. (2019). *Quantitative research methods for communication: A hands-on approach* (4th ed.). New York, NY: Oxford University Press.

Zimbardo, P. G. (1977). *Shyness: What it is, what to do about it.* Reading, MA: Addison-Wesley.

Zimbardo, P. G. (1981). *The shy child.* New York: McGraw-Hill.

Appendix A

Introversion Scale

Below are 18 statements that people sometimes make about themselves. Please indicate whether or not you believe each statement applies to you by marking whether you:

Strongly Disagree	Disagree	Neutral	Agree	Strongly Agree
1	2	3	4	5

_____ 1. Are you inclined to keep in the background on social occasions?

_____ 2. Do you like to mix socially with people?

_____ 3. Do you sometimes feel happy, sometimes depressed, without any apparent reason?

_____ 4. Are you inclined to limit your acquaintances to a select few?

_____ 5. Do you like to have many social engagements?

_____ 6. Do you have frequent ups and downs in mood, either with or without apparent cause?

_____ 7. Would you rate yourself as a happy-go-lucky individual?

_____ 8. Can you usually let yourself go and have a good time at a party?

_____ 9. Are you inclined to be moody?

_____10. Would you be very unhappy if you were prevented from making numerous social contacts?

_____11. Do you usually take the initiative in making new friends?

_____12. Does your mind often wander while you are trying to concentrate?

_____13. Do you like to play pranks upon others?

_____14. Are you usually a "good mixer"?

_____15. Are you sometimes bubbling over with energy and sometimes very sluggish?

_____16. Do you often "have the time of your life" at social affairs?

_____17. Are you frequently "lost in thought" even when you should be taking part in a conversation?

_____18. Do you derive more satisfaction from social activities than from anything else?

SCORING: To compute your scores follow the instructions below:

1. Introversion
   Step One: Add scores for items 1 and 4
   Step Two: Add the scores for items 2, 5, 7, 8, 10, 11, 13, 14, 16, and 18
   Step Three: Complete the following formula:

   Introversion = 12 − Total from Step 1 + Total from Step 2

Interpreting Your Score

Your score should be between 12 and 60. If you compute a score outside that range, you have made a mistake in computing the score. Note: Items 3, 6, 9, 12, 15, and 17 are not used in computing your introversion scale.

Individuals scoring above 48 are highly introverted; those scoring below 24 have low introversion (are extraverted). Those scoring between 24 and 48 are in the moderate range.

More Information

This introversion scale was developed by McCroskey to be distinct from measures of communication apprehension. An examination of the literature on introversion indicated that other introversions scales have included items that were tapping apprehension about communication. Items were drawn from the work of Eysenck, with items that referenced communication excluded. This permits the measurement of introversion without the contamination of communication apprehension items and allows the examination of both introversion and communication apprehension as predictors of communication behaviors independently of each other. The correlations of this measure with the PRCA-24 have been around .30. Alpha reliability estimates have been above .80. Items to measure neuroticism are used as filler items and are not scored with the introversion items.

Adapted from Eysenck, H. J. (1970). *Readings in extraversion-introversion: Volume I.* New York: Wiley-Interscience and Eysenck, H. J. (1971). *Readings in extraversion-introversion: Volume II.* New York: Wiley-Interscience.

Note: Items 3, 6, 9, 12, 15, and 17 are not scored. They are items recommended by Eysenck for measuring neuroticism.

Appendix B

Shyness Scale

Directions: Below are 14 statements that people sometimes make about themselves. Please indicate whether or not you believe each statement applies to you by marking whether you:

YES	yes	?	no	NO
1	2	3	4	5

_____ 1. I am a shy person.
_____ 2. Other people think I talk a lot.
_____ 3. I am a very talkative person.
_____ 4. Other people think I am shy.
_____ 5. I talk a lot.
_____ 6. I tend to be very quiet in class.
_____ 7. I don't talk much.
_____ 8. I talk more than most people.
_____ 9. I am a quiet person.
_____ 10. I talk more in a small group (3–6) than others do.
_____ 11. Most people talk more than I do.
_____ 12. Other people think I am very quiet.
_____ 13. I talk more in class than most people do.
_____ 14. Most people are more shy than I am.

SCORING: To compute your scores follow the instructions below:

1. Shyness
   Step One: Add scores for items 1, 4, 6, 7, 9, 11, and 12
   Step Two: Add scores for items 2, 3, 5, 8, 10, 13, and 14
   Step Three: Complete the following formula:

   Shyness = 42 + Total of Step 1 − Total of Step 2

Interpreting Your Score

Your score should be between 14 and 20. Scores above 52 indicate a high level of shyness. Scores below 32 indicate a low level of shyness. Scores between 32 and 52 indicate a moderate level of shyness.

More Information

This measure is also referred to as the McCroskey Shyness Scale. It was developed to obtain individual's self-report of his own shy behavior. Unlike many shyness scales that have been developed in the field of psychology, this scale does not confound communication apprehension with shy behavior. These are two very different constructs, and adding items from both provides an uninterpretable score. CA relates to fear and/or anxiety about communicating. Willingness to Communicate (WTC) relates to an orientation to initiate communication. Shyness relates to the actual communication behavior of reduced talking. This measure has generated high alpha reliability estimates (>.90) and has excellent face validity. Research has indicated that it also has high predictive validity-distinct from either CA or WTC measures.

Adapted from McCroskey, J. C., & Richmond, V. P. (1982). Communication apprehension and shyness: Conceptual and operational distinctions. *Central States Speech Journal, 33,* 458–468.

Willingness to Communicate Scale (WTC)

Directions: Below are 20 situations in which a person might choose to communicate or not to communicate. Presume you have **completely free choice**. Determine the percentage of times you would **choose to initiate communication** in each type of situation. Indicate in the space at the left what percent of the time you would chose to communicate. Choose any numbers between 0 and 100.

_____ 1. Talk with a service station attendant.
_____ 2. Talk with a physician.
_____ 3. Present a talk to a group of strangers.
_____ 4. Talk with an acquaintance while standing in line.
_____ 5. Talk with a salesperson in a store.
_____ 6. Talk in a large meeting of friends.
_____ 7. Talk with a police officer.
_____ 8. Talk in a small group of strangers.
_____ 9. Talk with a friend while standing in line.
_____10. Talk with a waiter/waitress in a restaurant.
_____11. Talk in a large meeting of acquaintances.
_____12. Talk with a stranger while standing in line.
_____13. Talk with a secretary.
_____14. Present a talk to a group of friends.
_____15. Talk in a small group of acquaintances.
_____16. Talk with a garbage collector.
_____17. Talk in a large meeting of strangers.
_____18. Talk with a spouse (or girl/boyfriend).
_____19. Talk in a small group of friends.
_____20. Present a talk to a group of acquaintances.

SCORING: The WTC permits computation of one total score and seven subscores. The range for all scores is 0 to 100. Follow the procedures outlined below.

1. Group discussion: Add scores for items 8, 15, and 19; divide sum by 3. Scores above 89 = high WTC; scores below 57 = low WTC in this context.
2. Meetings: Add scores for items 6, 11, and 17; divide sum by 3. Scores above 80 = high WTC; scores below 39 = low WTC in this context.
3. Interpersonal: Add scores for items 4, 9, and 12; divide sum by 3. Scores above 94 = high WTC; scores below 64 = low WTC in this context.
4. Public speaking: Add scores for items 3, 14, and 20; divide sum by 3. Scores above 78 = high WTC; scores below 33 = low WTC in this context.
5. Stranger: Add scores for items 3, 8, 12, and 17; divide sum by 4. Scores above 63 = high WTC; scores below 18 = low WTC with these receivers.
6. Acquaintance: Add scores for items 4, 11, 15, and 20; divide sum by 4. Scores above 92 = high WTC; scores below 57 = low WTC with these receivers.
7. Friends: Add scores for items 6, 9, 14, and 19; divide sum by 4. Scores above 99 = high WTC; scores below 71 = low WTC with these receivers.

To compute the total score for the WTC, add the totals for stranger, friend, and acquaintance, then divide by 3. Scores above 82 = high WTC; below 52 = low WTC.

Adapted from McCroskey, J. C. (1992). Reliability and validity of the willingness to communicate scale. *Communication Quarterly, 40*, 16–25.

Group Discussion	>89 High WTC, <57 Low WTC
Meetings	>80 High WTC, <39 Low WTC
Interpersonal Conversations	>94 High WTC, <64 Low WTC
Public Speaking	>78 High WTC, <33 Low WTC
Stranger	>63 High WTC, <18 Low WTC
Acquaintance	>92 High WTC, <57 Low WTC
Friend	>99 High WTC, <71 Low WTC
Total WTC	>82 High Overall WTC
	<52 Low Overall WTC

Writing Anxiety Scale (WAS)

Below are a series of statements about writing. There are no right or wrong answers to these statements. Although some of the statements below may seem repetitious, take your time and try to be as honest as possible. Please indicate the degree to which each of the following statement applies to you by marking whether you:

Strongly Disagree	Disagree	Neutral	Agree	Strongly Agree
1	2	3	4	5

_____ 1. When I stare at a blank screen, my mind goes blank and I don't
_____ know what to write.

_____ 2. Writing causes me a lot of anxiety.

_____ 3. Writing is not a pleasurable activity for me.

_____ 4. I do everything I can to avoid writing.

_____ 5. Whether writing an e-mail or a long paper/report, I generally experience a feeling of fear.

_____ 6. I don't think anyone really wants to read what I've written.

_____ 7. I experience a lot of nervousness when I start to write anything.

8. I do not feel confident in my ability to express my thoughts while
_____ writing.

_____ 9. I don't write as well as my peers.

_____ 10. I regularly experience "writers block" when I start writing.

SCORING: To compute your scores follow the instructions below:

1. Writing Anxiety

   Add items 1 to 10.

Interpreting Your Score

Scores should be between 10 and 50. If your score is below 10 or above 50, you have made a mistake. See discussion in Chapter 3 on "The Nature of Communication Apprehension" for interpretation of WAT scores.

Inspired by Daly, J. A., & Miller, M. D. (1975). The empirical development of an instrument to measure writing apprehension. *Research in the Teaching of English, 9,* 242–249.

Appendix E

Singing Anxiety Test (SAT)

Read the following questions and select the answer that corresponds with how you feel singing in front of other people. Do not be concerned if some of the items appear similar. Please use the scale below to rate the degree to which each statement applies to you:

Strongly Disagree	Disagree	Neutral	Agree	Strongly Agree
1	2	3	4	5

_____ 1. Singing in front of other people makes me nervous.

_____ 2. I experience no anxiety when I am asked to sing in front of an audience.

_____ 3. Even the idea of singing in front of other people makes me anxious.

_____ 4. I am completely uncomfortable with singing in front of anyone.

_____ 5. I become embarrassed any time I am asked to sing in front of others.

_____ 6. I have no problem with nerves when I sing in front of other people

_____ 7. I get anxiety when I am asked to sing in front of a group of people.

_____ 8. I experience no anxiety singing in front of a group of people.

_____ 9. I am completely relaxed when I sing in front of other people.

_____10. I experience great joy singing in front of an audience.

SCORING: To compute your scores follow the instructions below:

1. Singing Anxiety
    Step One: Add the scores for items 1, 3, 4, 5, and 7.
    Step Two: Add the scores for items 13 and 16.
    Step Three: Complete the following formula:

    SAT = 36 + Total from Step 1 − Total from Step 2.

Interpreting Your Score

Your score should be between 10 and 50. If your score is below 10 or above 50 you have made a mistake in computing the score. Most people will score below 30 on this scale. If you score between 30 and 39, you experience borderline singing anxiety levels. If your score is above 40, you definitely experience singing anxiety and singing in a choir with others or just singing karaoke at a local hot-spot is probably an unbelievably nerve-wracking experience.

Inspired by: Andersen, P. A., Andersen, J. F., & Garrison, J. P. (1978). Sing apprehension and talking apprehension: The development of two constructs. *Sign Language Studies, 19,* 155–186.

Personal Report of Communication Apprehension-24 (PRCA-24)

Directions: This instrument is composed of 24 statements concerning feelings about communicating with other people. Please indicate the degree to which each statement applies to you by marking whether you (1) strongly agree, (2) agree, (3) are undecided, (4) disagree, or (5) strongly disagree. Work quickly; record your first impression.

_____ 1. I dislike participating in group discussions.

_____ 2. Generally, I am comfortable while participating in group discussions.

_____ 3. I am tense and nervous while participating in group discussions.

_____ 4. I like to get involved in group discussions.

_____ 5. Engaging in a group discussion with new people makes me tense and nervous.

_____ 6. I am calm and relaxed while participating in group discussions.

_____ 7. Generally, I am nervous when I have to participate in a meeting.

_____ 8. Usually I am calm and relaxed while participating in meetings.

_____ 9. I am very calm and relaxed when I am called upon to express an opinion at a meeting.

_____ 10. I am afraid to express myself at meetings.

_____ 11. Communicating at meetings usually makes me uncomfortable.

_____ 12. I am very relaxed when answering questions at a meeting.

_____ 13. While participating in a conversation with a new acquaintance, I feel very nervous.

_____ 14. I have no fear of speaking up in conversations.

_____ 15. Ordinarily, I am very tense and nervous in conversations.

_____ 16. While conversing with a new acquaintance, I feel very relaxed.

_____ 17. Ordinarily, I am very calm and relaxed in conversations.

_____ 18. I'm afraid to speak up in conversations.

_____ 19. I have no fear of giving a speech.

_____ 20. Certain parts of my body feel very tense and rigid while I am giving a speech.

_____ 21. I feel relaxed while giving a speech.

_____ 22. My thoughts become confused and jumbled when I am giving a speech.

_____ 23. I face the prospect of giving a speech with confidence.

_____ 24. While giving a speech, I get so nervous I forget facts I really know.

Computing Score for PRCA-24

SCORING: To compute context subscores begin with a score of 18 for each context and follow the instructions below.

1. Group discussion: Add scores for items 2, 4, and 6. Subtract scores for items 1, 3, and 5. Scores can range from 6 to 30.
2. Meetings: Add scores for items 8, 9, and 12. Subtract scores for items 7, 10, and 11. Scores can range from 6 to 30.
3. Interpersonal: Add scores for items 14, 16, and 17. Subtract scores for items 13, 15, and 18. Scores can range from 6 to 30.
4. Public speaking: Add scores for items 19, 21, and 23. Subtract scores for items 20, 22, and 24. Scores can range from 6 to 30.

To compute the total score for the PRCA-24, add the four subscores. Total scores can range from 24 to 120. Scores above 80 = high CA; below 50 = low CA.

Adapted from McCroskey, J. C. (1982). *An introduction to rhetorical communication* (4th Ed). Englewood Cliffs, NJ: Prentice-Hall.

Norms for the PRCA-24		
	Mean	**Standard Deviation**
For Total Score	65.6	15.3
Group	15.4	4.8
Meeting	16.4	4.8
Dyad (Interpersonal)	14.5	4.2
Public	19.3	5.1

Appendix G

Personal Report of Public Speaking Anxiety (PRPSA)

Below are 34 statements that people sometimes make about themselves. Please indicate whether or not you believe each statement applies to you by marking whether you:

Strongly Disagree	Disagree	Neutral	Agree	Strongly Agree
1	2	3	4	5

_____ 1. While preparing for giving a speech, I feel tense and nervous.

_____ 2. I feel tense when I see the words "speech" and "public speech" on a course outline when studying.

_____ 3. My thoughts become confused and jumbled when I am giving a speech.

_____ 4. Right after giving a speech I feel that I have had a pleasant experience.

_____ 5. I get anxious when I think about a speech coming up.

_____ 6. I have no fear of giving a speech.

_____ 7. Although I am nervous just before starting a speech, I soon settle down after starting and feel calm and comfortable.

_____ 8. I look forward to giving a speech.

_____ 9. When the instructor announces a speaking assignment in class, I can feel myself getting tense.

_____10. My hands tremble when I am giving a speech.

_____11. I feel relaxed while giving a speech.

_____12. I enjoy preparing for a speech.

_____13. I am in constant fear of forgetting what I prepared to say.

_____14. I get anxious if someone asks me something about my topic that I don't know.

_____15. I face the prospect of giving a speech with confidence.

_____ 16. I feel that I am in complete possession of myself while giving a speech.

_____ 17. My mind is clear when giving a speech.

_____ 18. I do not dread giving a speech.

_____ 19. I perspire just before starting a speech.

_____ 20. My heart beats very fast just as I start a speech.

_____ 21. I experience considerable anxiety while sitting in the room just before my speech starts.

_____ 22. Certain parts of my body feel very tense and rigid while giving a speech.

_____ 23. Realizing that only a little time remains in a speech makes me tense and anxious.

_____ 24. While giving a speech, I know I can control my feelings of tension and stress.

_____ 25. I breathe faster just before starting a speech.

_____ 26. I feel comfortable and relaxed in the hour or so just before giving a speech.

_____ 27. I do poorer on speeches because I am anxious.

_____ 28. I feel anxious when the teacher announces the date of a speaking assignment.

_____ 29. When I make a mistake while giving a speech, I find it hard to concentrate on the parts that follow.

_____ 30. During an important speech I experience a feeling of helplessness building up inside me.

_____ 31. I have trouble falling asleep the night before a speech.

_____ 32. My heart beats very fast while I present a speech.

_____ 33. I feel anxious while waiting to give my speech.

_____ 34. While giving a speech, I get so nervous I forget facts I really know.

SCORING: To compute your scores follow the instructions below:

1. Public Speaking Anxiety
   Step One: Add scores for items 1, 2, 3, 5, 9, 10, 13, 14, 19, 20, 21, 22, 23, 25, 27, 28, 29, 30, 31, 32, 33, and 34
   Step Two: Add scores for items 4, 6, 7, 8, 11, 12, 15, 16, 17, 18, 24, and 26
   Step Three: Complete the following formula:

   PRPSA = 72 − Total from Step 2 + Total from Step 1

Interpreting Your Score

Your score should be between 34 and 170. If your score is below 34 or above 170, you have made a mistake in computing the score.

High = > 131
Low = < 98
Moderate = 98 to 131
Mean = 114.6; SD = 17.2

Adapted from McCroskey, J. C. (1970). Measures of communication-bound anxiety. *Speech Monographs, 37,* 269–277.

Appendix H

Communication Apprehension in Generalized Contexts

Communication Apprehension in Generalized Contexts

Below are 50 statements that people sometimes make about themselves. Please indicate whether or not you believe each statement applies to you by marking whether you:

Strongly Disagree	Disagree	Neutral	Agree	Strongly Agree
1	2	3	4	5

General

_____ 1. When communicating, I am generally calm and relaxed.
_____ 2. Generally, communication causes me to be anxious and apprehensive.
_____ 3. I find the prospect of speaking mildly pleasant.
_____ 4. When communicating, my posture feels strained and unnatural.
_____ 5. In general, communication makes me uncomfortable.
_____ 6. For the most part, I like to communicate with other people.
_____ 7. I dislike using my body and voice expressively.
_____ 8. I feel that I am more fluent when talking to people than most other people are.
_____ 9. When communicating, I generally am tense and nervous.
_____ 10. I feel relaxed and comfortable while speaking.

Group Discussions

_____ 11. I am afraid to express myself in a group.
_____ 12. I dislike participating in group discussions.
_____ 13. Generally, I am comfortable while participating in group discussions.

_____ 14. I am tense and nervous while participating in group discussions.

_____ 15. I have no fear about expressing myself in a group.

_____ 16. Engaging in a group discussion with new people is pleasant.

_____ 17. Generally, I am uncomfortable while participating in a group discussion.

_____ 18. I like to get involved in group discussions.

_____ 19. Engaging in a group discussion with new people makes me tense and nervous.

_____ 20. I am calm and relaxed while participating in group discussions.

Meetings

_____ 21. I look forward to expressing my opinions at meetings.

_____ 22. I am self-conscious when I am called upon to express an opinion at a meeting.

_____ 23. Generally, I am nervous when I have to participate in a meeting.

_____ 24. Communicating in meetings generally makes me feel good.

_____ 25. Usually, I am calm and relaxed while participating in meetings.

_____ 26. I am self-conscious when I am called upon to answer a question at a meeting.

_____ 27. I am very calm and relaxed when I am called upon to express an opinion at a meeting.

_____ 28. I am afraid to express myself at meetings.

_____ 29. Communicating in meetings generally makes me feel uncomfortable.

_____ 30. I am very relaxed when answering questions at a meeting.

Interpersonal Conversations

_____ 31. While participating in a conversation with a new acquaintance, I feel very nervous.

_____ 32. I have no fear of speaking up in conversations.

_____ 33. Talking with one other person very often makes me nervous.

_____ 34. Ordinarily, I am very tense and nervous in conversations.

_____ 35. Conversing with people who hold positions of authority causes me to be fearful and tense.

_____ 36. Generally, I am very relaxed while talking with one other person.

_____ 37. Ordinarily, I am very calm and relaxed in conversations.

_____ 38. While conversing with a new acquaintance, I feel very relaxed.

_____ 39. I am relaxed while conversing with people who hold positions of authority.

_____ 40. I am afraid to speak up in conversations.

Public Speeches

_____ 41. I have no fear of giving a speech.

_____ 42. I look forward to giving a speech.

_____ 43. Certain parts of my body feel very tense and rigid while giving a speech.

_____ 44. I feel relaxed while giving a speech.

_____ 45. Giving a speech makes me anxious.

_____ 46. My thoughts become confused and jumbled when I am giving a speech.

_____ 47. I face the prospect of giving a speech with confidence.

_____ 48. While giving a speech, I get so nervous I forget facts I really know.

_____ 49. Giving a speech really scares me.

_____ 50. While giving a speech, I know I can control my feelings of tension and stress.

SCORING: To compute your scores follow the instructions below:

General = 30 − (total of items 2, 4, 5, 7, 9) + (total of items 1, 3, 6, 8, 10)

Group = 30 − (total of items 11, 12, 14, 17, 19) + (total of items 13, 15, 16, 18, 20)

Meetings = 30 − (total of items 22, 23, 26, 28, 29) + (total of items 21, 24, 25, 27, 30)

Interpersonal = 30 − (total of items 31, 33, 34, 35, 40) + (total of items 32, 36, 37, 38, 39)

Public = 30 − (total of items 43, 45, 46, 48, 49) + (total of items 41, 42, 44, 47, 50)

Interpreting Your Score

See the discussion in Chapter 3 on "Context-Based Communication Apprehension for interpretation of results.

Adapted from Richmond, V. P., & McCroskey, J. C. (1995). _Communication: Apprehension, avoidance, and effectiveness_ (4th ed.). Scarsdale, AZ: Gorsuch Scarisbrick.

Appendix I

Situational Communication Apprehension Measure (SCAM)

Please complete the following questionnaire about how you felt **the last time you interacted with someone who had a supervisory role over you**. There are no right or wrong answers. Just respond to the items quickly to describe as accurately as you can how you felt while interacting with that person.

Extremely inaccurate	Moderately inaccurate	Somewhat accurate	Neither accurate nor inaccurate	Somewhat accurate	Moderately accurate	Extremely accurate
1	2	3	4	5	6	7

_____ 1. I was apprehensive
_____ 2. I was disturbed
_____ 3. I felt peaceful
_____ 4. I was loose
_____ 5. I felt uneasy
_____ 6. I was self-assured
_____ 7. I was fearful
_____ 8. I was ruffled
_____ 9. I felt jumpy
_____ 10. I was composed

_____ 11. I was bothered
_____ 12. I felt satisfied
_____ 13. I felt safe
_____ 14. I was flustered
_____ 15. I was cheerful
_____ 16. I felt happy
_____ 17. I felt dejected
_____ 18. I was pleased
_____ 19. I felt good
_____ 20. I was unhappy

SCORING: To compute your scores follow the instructions below:

1. SCAM

   Step One: Add scores for items 3, 4, 6, 10, 12, 13, 15, 16, 18, and 19
   Step Two: Add scores for items 1, 2, 5, 7, 8, 9, 11, 14, 17, and 20
   Step Three: Complete the following formula:

   SCAM = 80 − Total from Step 1 + Total from Step 2

Interpreting Your Score

Your score should be between 20 and 140. If your score is below 20 or above 140, you have made a mistake in computing the score.

There are no norms for this measure, since different contexts will generate different score ranges, means, and standard deviations. The Situational Communication Apprehension Measure was developed to provide an instrument that could measure state CA in any context. This is a self-report instrument that can apply to how a person felt in any recent communication event (the closer in time between the event and completion of this instrument, the more valid the measure will be). In the example below, in the directions we describe the communication context as "the last time you interacted with someone who had a supervisory role over you." This may be replaced by any other context, for example, "talked with one of your subordinates," "talked with your teacher outside class," "met with your physician."

Adapted from Richmond, V. P. (1978). The relationship between trait and state communication apprehension and interpersonal perception during acquaintance stages. *Human Communication Research, 4,* 338–349.

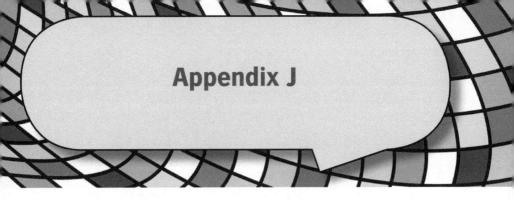

Appendix J

Self-Perceived Communication Competence (SPCC)

Directions: Below are 12 situations in which you might need to communicate. People's abilities to communicate effectively vary, and sometimes the same person is more competent to communicate in one situation than in another. Please indicate how competent you believe you are to communicate in each of the situations described below. Indicate in the space provided at the left of each item your estimate of your competence.

Presume 0 = completely incompetent; 100 = competent.

_____ 1. Present a talk to a group of strangers.
_____ 2. Talk with an acquaintance.
_____ 3. Talk in a large meeting of friends.
_____ 4. Talk in a small group of strangers.
_____ 5. Talk with a friend.
_____ 6. Talk in a large meeting of acquaintances.
_____ 7. Talk with a stranger.
_____ 8. Present a talk to a group of friends.
_____ 9. Talk in a small group of acquaintances.
_____10. Talk in a large meeting of strangers.
_____11. Talk in a small group of friends.
_____12. Present a talk to a group of acquaintances.

Scoring: To compute the subscores, add the percentages for the items indicated and divide the total by the number indicated below.

Public	1 + 8 + 12; divide by 3.
Meeting	3 + 6 + 10; divide by 3.
Group	4 + 9 + 11; divide by 3.
Dyad	2 + 5 + 7; divide by 3.

Stranger   1 + 4 + 7 + 10; divide by 4.
Acquaintance   2 + 6 + 9 + 12; divide by 4.
Friend   3 + 5 + 8 + 11; divide by 4.

Public	>86 High SPCC	<51 Low SPCC
Meeting	>85 High SPCC	<51 Low SPCC
Group	>90 High SPCC	<61 Low SPCC
Dyad	>93 High SPCC	<68 Low SPCC
Stranger	>79 High SPCC	<31 Low SPCC
Acquaintance	>92 High SPCC	<62 Low SPCC
Friend	>99 High SPCC	<76 Low SPCC
Total	>87 High SPCC	<59 Low SPCC

Higher SPCC scores indicate higher self-perceived communication competence with basic communication contexts (public, meeting, group, dyad) and receivers (strangers, acquaintance, friend).

Adapted from McCroskey, J. C., & McCroskey, L. L. (1988). Self-report as an approach to measuring communication competence. *Communication Research Reports, 5,* 108–113.

Talkaholism or Compulsive Communication

The questionnaire below includes 16 statements about talking behavior. Please indicate the degree to which you believe each of these characteristics applies to you by marking, on the line before each item, whether you:

Strongly Disagree	Disagree	Neutral	Agree	Strongly Agree
1	2	3	4	5

There are no right or wrong answers. Work quickly; record your first impression.

_____ 1. Often I keep quiet when I know I should talk.

_____ 2. I talk more than I should sometimes.

_____ 3. Often, I talk when I know I should keep quiet.

_____ 4. Sometimes I keep quiet when I know it would be to my advantage to talk.

_____ 5. I am a "talkaholic."

_____ 6. Sometimes I feel compelled to keep quiet.

_____ 7. In general, I talk more than I should.

_____ 8. I am a compulsive talker.

_____ 9. I am not a talker; rarely do I talk in communication situations.

_____ 10. Quite a few people have said I talk too much.

_____ 11. I just can't stop talking too much.

_____ 12. In general, I talk less than I should.

_____ 13. I am *not* a "talkaholic."

_____ 14. Sometimes I talk when I know it would be to my advantage to keep quiet.

_____ 15. I talk less than I should sometimes.

_____ 16. I am *not* a compulsive talker.

SCORING: To determine your score on this scale, complete the following steps:

Step 1.   Add the scores for items 2, 3, 5, 7, 8, 10, 11, and 14.
Step 2.   Add the scores for items 13 and 16.
Step 3.   Complete the following formula:

Talkaholic score = 12 + total from Step 1 − total from step 2.

People who score between 30 and 39 are borderline talkaholics and are able to control their talking most of the time, but sometimes they find themselves in situations where it is difficult to be quiet, even if it would be very much to their advantage not to talk. People with scores above 40 are talkaholics.

Adapted from McCroskey, J. C., & Richmond, V. P. (1993). Identifying compulsive communicators: The talkaholic scale. *Communication Research Reports, 11*, 39–52 and

McCroskey, J. C., & Richmond, V. P. (1995). Correlates of compulsive communication: Quantitative and qualitative characteristics. *Communication Quarterly, 43*, 39–52.

Personal Report of Intercultural Communication Apprehension (PRICA)

The 14 statements below are comments frequently made by people with regard to communication with people from other cultures. Please indicate how much you agree with these statements by marking a number representing your response to each statement using the following choices:

Strongly Disagree	Disagree	Neutral	Agree	Strongly Agree
1	2	3	4	5

_____ 1. Generally, I am comfortable interacting with a group of people from different cultures.

_____ 2. I am tense and nervous while interacting with people from different cultures.

_____ 3. I like to get involved in group discussion with others who are from different cultures.

_____ 4. Engaging in a group discussion with people from different cultures makes me nervous.

_____ 5. I am calm and relaxed with interacting with a group of people who are from different cultures.

_____ 6. While participating in a conversation with a person from a different culture, I get nervous.

_____ 7. I have no fear of speaking up in a conversation with a person from a different culture.

_____ 8. Ordinarily, I am very tense and nervous in a conversation with a person from a different culture.

_____ 9. Ordinarily, I am very calm and relaxed in conversations with a person from a different culture.

_____10. While conversing with a person from a different culture, I feel very relaxed.

_____11. I am afraid to speak up in conversations with a person from a different culture.

_____12. I face the prospect of interacting with people from different cultures with confidence.

_____13. My thoughts become confused and jumbled when interacting with people from different cultures.

_____14. Communicating with people from different cultures makes me feel uncomfortable.

SCORING: To compute your scores follow the instructions below:

1. PRICA
   Step One: Add scores for items 1, 3, 5, 7, 9, 10, and 12
   Step Two: Add scores for items 2, 4, 6, 8, 11, 13, and 14
   Step Three: Complete the following formula:

PRICA score = 42 − Total from Step 1 + Total from Step 2

Interpreting Your Score

Scores can range from 14 to 70. Scores below 32 indicate low intercultural CA. Scores above 52 indicate high intercultural CA. Scores ranging between 32 and 52 indicate a moderate level of intercultural CA.

Adapted from Neuliep, J. W., & McCroskey, J. C. (1997). The development of intercultural and interethnic communication apprehension scales. *Communication Research Reports, 14,* 385–398.

Appendix M

Personal Report of Interethnic Communication Apprehension (PRECA)

Below are items that relate to the cultures of different parts of the world. Work quickly and record your first reaction to each item. There are no right or wrong answers. Please indicate the degree to which you agree or disagree with each item using the following five-point scale:

Strongly Disagree	Disagree	Neutral	Agree	Strongly Agree
1	2	3	4	5

_____ 1. I dislike interacting with people from different ethnic/racial groups.

_____ 2. Generally, I am comfortable interacting with a group of people from different ethnic/racial groups.

_____ 3. I am tense and nervous while interacting with people from different ethnic/racial groups.

_____ 4. I like to get involved in group discussions with others who are from different ethnic/racial groups.

_____ 5. Engaging in a group discussion with people from different ethnic/racial groups makes me nervous.

_____ 6. I am calm and relaxed with interacting with a group of people who are from different ethnic/racial groups.

_____ 7. While participating in a conversation with a person from a different ethnic/racial group, I get nervous.

_____ 8. I have no fear of speaking up in a conversation with a person from a different ethnic/racial group.

_____ 9. Ordinarily, I am very tense and nervous in a conversation with a person from a different ethnic/racial group.

_____10. Ordinarily, I am very calm and relaxed in conversations with a person from a different ethnic/racial group.

_____11. While conversing with a person from a different ethnic/racial group, I feel very relaxed.

_____12. I'm afraid to speak up in conversations with a person from a different ethnic/racial group.

_____13. I face the prospect of interacting with people from different ethnic/racial groups with confidence.

_____14. My thoughts become confused and jumbled when interacting with people from different ethnic/racial groups.

_____15. I enjoy interacting with people from different ethnic/racial groups.

_____16. Communicating with people from different ethnic/racial groups makes me feel uncomfortable.

SCORING: To compute your scores follow the instructions below:

1. PRECA
   Step One: Add scores for items 1, 3, 5, 7, 9, 12, 14, and 16
   Step Two: Add scores for items 2, 4, 6, 8, 10, 11, 13, and 15
   Step Three: Complete the following formula:

   PRECA = 48 − Step 1 + Step 2

Interpreting Your Score

Scores can range from 14 to 70. Scores below 32 indicate low interethnic CA. Scores above 52 indicate high interethnic CA. Scores ranging between 32 and 52 indicate a moderate level of interethnic CA.

Adapted from Neuliep, J.W., & McCroskey, J.C. (1997). The development of intercultural and interethnic communication apprehension scales. *Communication Research Reports, 14*, 385–398.

Religious Communication Apprehension (RCA)

Please circle the number that best represents your feelings. The closer a number is to the item/adjective the more you feel that way.
Overall, the instructor I have in the class is:

1.	Safe	1 2 3 4 5 6 7	Uneasy
2.	Peaceful	1 2 3 4 5 6 7	Fearful
3.	Flustered	7 6 5 4 3 2 1	Organized
4.	Peaceful	1 2 3 4 5 6 7	Disturbed
5.	Anxious	7 6 5 4 3 2 1	Calm
6.	Uneasy	7 6 5 4 3 2 1	Sure
7.	Self-Assured	1 2 3 4 5 6 7	Unsure
8.	Ruffled	7 6 5 4 3 2 1	Unruffled
9.	Nervous	7 6 5 4 3 2 1	Composed
10.	Apprehensive	7 6 5 4 3 2 1	Nonapprehensive

Scoring:
Add all of the numbers you circled together.

Interpretation

Scores should be between 10 and 70. Higher scores indicate higher levels of religious communication apprehension. Scores above 52 indicate high religious CA. Scores ranging between 32 and 52 indicate a moderate level of religious CA.

Adapted from Punyanunt-Carter, N. M., Wrench, J. C., Corrigan, M. W., & McCroskey, J. C. (2008). An examination of reliability and validity of the Religious Communication Apprehension Scale. *Journal of Intercultural Communication Research, 37,* 1–15. doi: 10.1080/174757080277339

Appendix O

Sociocommunicative Orientation

Directions: The questionnaire below lists 20 personality characteristics. Please indicate the degree to which you believe each of these characteristics applies to YOU, as you normally communicate with others, by marking whether you (5) strongly agree that it applies, (4) agree that it applies, (3) are undecided, (2) disagree that it applies, or (1) strongly disagree that it applies. There are no right or wrong answers. Work quickly; record your first impression.

_____ 1. helpful
_____ 2. defends own beliefs
_____ 3. independent
_____ 4. responsive to others
_____ 5. forceful
_____ 6. has strong personality
_____ 7. sympathetic
_____ 8. compassionate
_____ 9. assertive
_____ 10. sensitive to the needs of others
_____ 11. dominant
_____ 12. sincere
_____ 13. gentle
_____ 14. willing to take a stand
_____ 15. warm
_____ 16. tender
_____ 17. friendly
_____ 18. acts as a leader
_____ 19. aggressive
_____ 20. competitive

*Items 2,3,5,6,9,11,14,18,19, and 20 measure assertiveness. Add the scores on these items to get your assertiveness score. Items 1,4,7,8,10,12,13,15,16, and 17 measure responsiveness. Add the scores on these items to get your responsiveness score.

Adapted from Richmond, V. P., & McCroskey, J. C. (1990). Reliability and separation of factors on the assertiveness-responsiveness scale. *Psychological Reports, 67,* 449–450.

Appendix P

Fear of Physician (FOP)

The five statements below are common comments made by patients concerning their physicians. Please indicate in the space before each item how you feel when communicating with your physician. Please indicate how well each statement describes how you feel when communicating your physician employing the following scale:

not at all	somewhat	moderately so	very much so
1	2	3	4

_____ 1. When communicating with my physician, I feel tense.
_____ 2. When communicating with my physician, I feel calm.
_____ 3. When communicating with my physician, I feel jittery.
_____ 4. When communicating with my physician, I feel nervous.
_____ 5. When communicating with my physician, I feel relaxed.

SCORING: To compute your scores follow the instructions below:

1. Fear of Physician
   Step One: Add scores for items 1, 3, and 4
   Step Two: Add scores for items 2 and 5
   Step Three: Complete the following formula:

   FOP = 15 + total for Step 1 − total for Step 2

Interpreting Your Score

Scores above 13 indicates high fear of physician. Scores below 7 indicate low fear of physician. Scores between 7 and 13 indicate moderate fear of physician.

Adapted from Richmond, V. P., Smith, R. S., Jr., Heisel, A. M., & McCroskey, J. C. (1998). The impact of communication apprehension and fear of talking with a physician on perceived medical outcomes. *Communication Research Reports, 15,* 344–353.

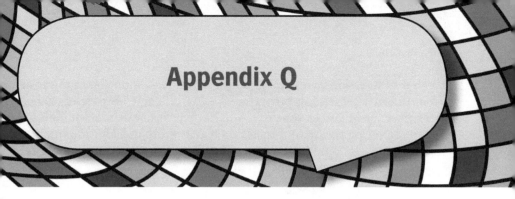

Appendix Q

Computer-Mediated Communication Apprehension (CMCA)

This set of questions asks you about how you feel while communicating using e-mail. If you have never used e-mail, please leave this section blank. Work quickly and indicate your first impression. Please indicate the degree to which each statement applies to you by marking whether you:

Strongly Disagree	Disagree	Neutral	Agree	Strongly Agree
1	2	3	4	5

_____ 1. When communicating using e-mail, I feel tense.

_____ 2. When communicating using e-mail, I feel calm.

_____ 3. When communicating using e-mail, I feel jittery.

_____ 4. When communicating using e-mail, I feel nervous.

_____ 5. When communicating using e-mail, I feel relaxed.

This set of questions asks you about how you feel while communicating in online chat rooms, IRCs, or MUDDS. If you have never used chat rooms, IRCs, or MUDDS, please leave this section blank. Work quickly and indicate your first impression. Please indicate the degree to which each statement applies to you by marking whether you:

Strongly Disagree	Disagree	Neutral	Agree	Strongly Agree
1	2	3	4	5

_____ 6. When communicating in a chat room, IRC, or MUDD, I feel tense.

_____ 7. When communicating in a chat room, IRC, or MUDD, I feel calm.

_____ 8. When communicating in a chat room, IRC, or MUDD, I feel jittery.

_____ 9. When communicating in a chat room, IRC, or MUDD, I feel nervous.

_____10. When communicating in a chat room, IRC, or MUDD, I feel relaxed.

This set of questions asks you about how you feel while communicating using Internet messaging programs like AOL Instant Messenger, Yahoo Messenger, or MSN Messenger. If you have never used Internet messaging programs, please leave this section blank. Work quickly, and indicate your first impression. Please indicate the degree to which each statement applies to you by marking whether you:

Strongly Disagree	Disagree	Neutral	Agree	Strongly Agree
1	2	3	4	5

_____11. When communicating using an Internet messaging program, I feel tense.

_____12. When communicating using an Internet messaging program, I feel calm.

_____13. When communicating using an Internet messaging program, I feel jittery.

_____14. When communicating using an Internet messaging program, I feel nervous.

_____15. When communicating using an Internet messaging program, I feel relaxed.

SCORING: To compute your scores follow the instructions below:

1. E-mail Apprehension
   Step One: Add scores for items 1, 3, and 4
   Step Two: Add scores for items 2 and 5
   Step Three: Complete the following formula

   E-mail Apprehension = 15 + total for Step 1 − total for Step 2

2. Chatting Apprehension
   Step One: Add scores for items 6, 8, and 9
   Step Two: Add scores for items 7 and 10
   Step Three: Complete the following formula

   Chatting Apprehension = 15 + total for Step 1 − total for Step 2

3. Instant Messaging Apprehension
   Step One: Add scores for items 11, 13, and 14
   Step Two: Add scores for items 12 and 15
   Step Three: Complete the following formula

   E-mail Apprehension = 15 + total for Step 1 − total for Step 2

Interpreting Your Score

Scores on all three measures should be between 5 and 25. For e-mail apprehension, scores under 9.5 are considered low, and scores over 9.5 are considered high. For chatting apprehension, scores under 11.5 are considered low, and scores over 11.5 are considered high. For instant messaging apprehension, scores under 9 are considered low, and scores over 9 are considered high.

Adapted from Wrench, J. S., & Punyanunt-Carter, N. M. (2007). The relationship between computer-mediated-communication competence, apprehension, self-efficacy, perceived confidence, and social presence. *Southern Journal of Communication, 72,* 355–378. doi: 10.1080/10417940701667696